Killer
Psychopaths

Killer
Psychopaths

The inside story of criminal profiling

Paul Roland

PICTURE CREDITS

Akg-images: 50

Corbis: 31, 40, 78, 83, 86, 94, 101, 104, 108, 115, 133, 135, 151, 172, 205, 212

Getty Images: 91, 120, 139

PA Photos: 229, 232

Public Domain: 18, 49, 62, 68

Shutterstock: 187

Topfoto: 162, 199

Topham Picturepoint: 191

This edition published in 2021 by Arcturus Publishing Limited
26/27 Bickels Yard, 151–153 Bermondsey Street,
London SE1 3HA

AD008584UK

Printed in the UK

Contents

Foreword

Thousands of books have been written about murder and many others have been written about 'profiling', but the reader will find this book to be different from the others in several ways. To begin with, the author takes the reader through a historical tour of infamous offenders including terrorists, serial killers, assassins and dictators, explaining how different applications of 'profiling' have played an important role in the past. Second, it does not attempt to shock the reader with gory descriptions of gruesome crimes – rather it informs via factual presentations of case information. Third, it was written with the informed reader in mind and consequently is well researched in a variety of fields including history, psychology, sociology, and criminal investigative analysis or 'profiling'. Fourth, the author utilizes the works and words of recognized experts in the field. Experts in the sense of their having been members of the FBI's Behavioral Science Unit in the 'early days' and therefore possessing first hand information. Finally a fact very much appreciated by this writer, the author does not approach 'profiling' in a sensational manner but instead presents the topic in a straightforward way.

This book provides the reader with a wide variety of tasks assigned to FBI and other profilers which include research interviews, proactive strategies, crime analysis of staged crimes, linking of cases via behaviour, and interrogation. One feature of the book – something which will be of great interest to the reader – is a series of crime accounts and the responsible criminals against which the profiling process was successfully applied.

Having worked as a 'profiler' in the FBI's Behavioral Science Unit (1978–1994) and having continued in the same work with a group of retired FBI 'profilers' at the Academy Group, Inc. (AGI), it is my considered opinion that a close study of the investigative tool known as 'profiling' always reveals that it is much simpler than imagined. This book supports the truthfulness of that statement in a factual, informative, and enjoyable manner.

Roy Hazelwood

Introduction

Hearts of Darkness

'Criminals think differently from responsible people.'
Dr Stanton Samenow, *Inside the Criminal Mind*, 1984

This is not another book about serial killers, although you will find some of the most notorious mass murderers of modern times profiled in these pages, together with sexual sadists, serial rapists, arsonists, extortionists, bank robbers, war criminals, tyrants and terrorists.

Nor is it yet another rehash of famous cases that will be overly familiar to connoisseurs of true crime. It is far more interesting than that because this book explores the new art of criminal profiling and what it reveals about the nature of evil, specifically what motivates men, women and sometimes even children to commit the most appalling acts imaginable.

Offender profiling was largely but not exclusively developed by the FBI Behavioral Science Unit at Quantico, Virginia during the late 1970s and 1980s and is now widely practised throughout the world by law enforcement professionals who have come to realize that even forensic science is not infallible.

Profiles can be prospective which means that they can be used to predict which individuals in a particular segment of society have the potential to offend, or they can be retrospective which involves identifying which type of individual might have been responsible for a specific crime or series of crimes from the behaviour they exhibited at the scene. Prospective profiles are generally favoured by intelligence agencies who seek to identify potential terrorists before they commit an atrocity, but this approach is controversial and has come under increasing criticism because it can lead to racial stereotyping, whereas retrospective profiling aims to create a behavioural composite of an unknown subject or UNSUB, to narrow the focus of an investigation rather than pointing a finger at a specific individual.

Hundreds of cases each year in the United States alone benefit from the insights provided by BSU profilers who have been able to claim a 92 per cent accuracy rating every year between 1978 and 1994, according to Russell Vorpagel in *Profiles in Murder*. The standard FBI profile features 15 key points or clues to the type of personality who should be considered responsible for the offence. If two of these points prove to be inaccurate, the Bureau considers it one of their rare mistakes.

Former FBI Special Agent Vorpagel described the profiling process as a 'psychological autopsy' and compared the profile itself to an Impressionist painting which is composed of numerous brush strokes none of which may be significant on their own, but taken together create a meaningful picture.

Killer Psychopaths reveals the secrets of this new method, specifically how a profiler can tell when a crime scene has been staged or altered and whether a murder victim has been posed to divert attention from the intended offence, usually robbery or rape. It describes the extent to which fantasy and control compels sadistic offenders to abduct and torture total strangers, the significance of the serial killer's 'signature' and what part stressors play in pushing a perpetrator over the edge.

It details what the choice of weapon and ferocity of an attack reveal about the assailant, what can be gleaned from a body that has been mutilated post-mortem as well as what the manner of disposal and the location tell investigators about the killer's relationship to the victim. Was it simply dumped, partially covered or buried?

But the potential benefits of profiling are not limited to murder cases. An arsonist's choice of accelerant, the tone of an extortionist's letters and a hostage-taker's list of demands all help to disclose the type of person responsible for these crimes, their state of mind and the level of threat that they pose.

From the most seemingly insignificant clues, an experienced profiler can quickly determine the offender's sex, age, physical appearance, personal circumstances, background, occupation and even the model and condition of the car they drive. By recreating the crime from clues left at the scene it is also possible to predict the perpetrator's next move.

Using a mixture of behavioural analysis, personal experience and intuition, leading profilers such as the FBI's John Douglas, the inspiration for Special Agent Jack Crawford in *The Silence of the Lambs*, and England's real-life *Cracker*, Dr Paul Britton, can get inside the mind of a child molester or under the skin of a psychopath to devise strategies that can be used to track and trap these predators.

They can force an abductor to break cover and lead them to their captive; they can spot an arsonist in a crowd, or identify a likely member of a terrorist cell before they can carry out their threat to kill innocent people. They can even provoke the most determined extortionist into making the fatal error that will end their reign of terror. But they will be the first to dispel the myth that they catch criminals. That is the job of the police.

Profilers are instrumental in identifying the type of person who is likely to be responsible and they frequently prove to be uncannily accurate. But contrary to the impression created by popular television series such as *Millennium, Missing, Criminal Minds* and *Profiler* there is no psychic element to profiling. It is a method based on sound proven principles. There may be an element of intuition derived from years of experience, but when a profiler surveys the crime scene and puts himself or herself in the mind of the unknown subject, they are using psychology, not their sixth sense.

For the profiler the crime scene is a puzzle with only one piece missing – the identity of the offender. All of the remaining pieces are scattered at the scene. There are four steps in profiling the offender or offenders, four crucial questions which initiate every investigation: What happened? How did it happen (sequence of events)? Why did it happen? Who did it?

But despite its reputation for cracking the coldest of cold cases and solving the most intractable crimes, profiling has its limitations. It is of little use in identifying perpetrators of routine crimes such as street robberies because these offences are so common and the offender's behaviour is rarely unusual. Single high-risk victims such as prostitutes and those killed by a single shot or stab wound also offer little for the profiler to work with. And on a purely practical point, with an average of 25,000 murders in the US alone each year, there simply aren't enough experienced profilers to work on all the serious crimes they might be able to help solve.

A Confusion of Clues

Procedural police shows such as the phenomenally popular *CSI* have made even the amateur thief acutely aware of the value of trace evidence. Consequently today's criminals are becoming increasingly cunning at covering their tracks.

Once the CSIs have finished dusting for prints, scoured the crime scene for hair and fibres and swabbed surfaces for blood, semen and saliva they may be faced with too few clues and too many suspects. It is only on TV and in the movies that forensic technicians can analyze a single hair, fleck of paint or partial thumb print in a matter of minutes. In real life, even the most efficient, generously funded forensic laboratories can take months to process evidence if they are overwhelmed or understaffed. In one notable case (see page 226), it took almost two years to process over 200 DNA samples before the suspect was identified, by which time he had graduated from rape to abduction, torture and murder. In such cases, a profiler can help focus an investigation so that valuable police resources are not wasted, the most valuable of all, of course, being time.

But profiling is only part of a larger, more comprehensive behavioural assessment process known as Criminal Investigative Analysis which involves helping to provide probable cause in support of a search warrant, advising on interviewing techniques, trial strategy and threat assessment. In short, profiling does not end with the capture of the criminal. As the second chapter of this book reveals, profilers can perform a crucial role by devising interview strategies for coaxing an offender into making a full confession. Without it a multiple murderer might only be prosecuted for the crime for which the police have physical evidence and there is always the possibility that they could get off on a legal technicality, or by virtue of their lawyer introducing reasonable doubt. Criminals – and serial killers in particular – tend to be highly manipulative individuals who have perfected the art of deception and as such many are capable of feigning whatever mental disorder they believe will declare them unfit to stand trial or earn them a shorter sentence. Even if they fail the psych tests they may still fool the jury, which is where the profiler may be called in as an expert witness to strip aside the facade of feigned innocence and reveal the monster behind the mask. Profilers also provide assessments at parole hearings when a decision has to be made whether to release a potential re-offender back into society. This aspect of their work raises the perennial problem of whether or not sexual offenders and sadistic killers can ever be cured of their compulsion.

Killer Psychopaths reveals how the comparatively new method of criminal profiling is helping to catch and convict these predators by getting inside their minds and exploiting the flaw in their personality. It explodes the myth of the motiveless crime and the belief that all killers are crazy.

In the following pages you can learn how bank robbers choose their target, why extortionists want more than money and what the FBI learnt from their 50 face-to-face interviews with the most evil men on Earth, including a look inside the FBI's elite Behavioral Science Unit at Quantico, Virginia and how the Bureau train their profilers.

'Profiling the repeat murderer can be compared to a doctor's predictions regarding a patient's progress in a disease. Serial killers have a disease ... If a criminal profiler is told that a teenager is a bed-wetter, plays with matches and tortures animals, he can predict the potential for future sociopathic homicides. It's not magic, it's logic.'

FBI profiler Russell Vorpagel

Chapter One:
Footsteps in the Fog

'The sixth commandment – "Thou Shalt Not Kill" – fascinated me. I always knew that some day I should defy it.'

Reginald Halliday Christie, serial killer

'I was born with the devil in me. I could not help the fact that I was a murderer, no more than the poet can help the inspiration to sing ... I was born with the evil one standing as my sponsor beside the bed where I was ushered into the world, and he has been with me since.'

H. H. Holmes, America's original
serial killer, executed 1896

In the late 19th century, prior to the development of fingerprinting and ballistics, real-life detectives in Europe, Asia and America were putting Sherlock Holmes to shame with nothing more than a magnifying glass and their intellectual curiosity. At the same time psychiatric pioneers such as Richard von Krafft-Ebing were making the first forays into the dark recesses of the psyche in an attempt to understand mental disorders and aberrant sexual compulsions.

But all attempts at probing the criminal mind with a view to predicting behaviour were flawed by prejudices and presumptions. The French investigator Alphonse Bertillon (1853–1914) and the Italian criminologist Cesare Lombrosso (1836–1909), for example, asserted that criminality was either inherited or determined by an individual's physical characteristics. It wasn't until the first serial killer of modern times had driven the police to distraction that a serious attempt was made to comprehend the criminal personality in order to identify and apprehend an offender.

Jack the Ripper

One of the earliest recorded attempts to profile a serial killer was made in the autumn of 1888 by British police surgeon Dr Thomas Bond who had been asked to assist in the investigation into the Whitechapel murders in London attributed to Jack the Ripper.

Rumours were rife that the fiend was a medical man, and so it was given to Dr Bond to study the autopsy reports of the first four victims and make a comparison with his own findings on the fifth as to whether or not the mutilations revealed any medical knowledge. Sir Robert Anderson, the Metropolitan Police Commissioner, was under considerable public pressure to solve the case which had focused the eyes of the world on the squalid living conditions of the poor in the East End. And so it was with a sense of urgency that Anderson urged Dr Bond to use his experience to determine if there was any evidence to support the assumption that the killings were the work of one man. Bond submitted his report on 10 November, the day after he had performed the post-mortem examination on what we assume was the Ripper's final victim, Mary Kelly.

Psychosexual pioneer Richard von Krafft-Ebing with his wife.

'I beg to report that I have read the notes of the 4 Whitechapel
Murders viz:
1. Bucks Row.
2. Hanbury Street.
3. Berners Street.
4. Mitre Square.

I have also made a Post Mortem Examination of the mutilated
remains of a woman found yesterday in a small room in Dorset
Street –
1. All five murders were no doubt committed by the same hand.
   In the first four the throats appear to have been cut from left
   to right. In the last case owing to the extensive mutilation it
   is impossible to say in what direction the fatal cut was made,

but arterial blood was found on the wall in splashes close to where the woman's head must have been lying.

2. *All the circumstances surrounding the murders lead me to form the opinion that the women must have been lying down when murdered and in every case the throat was first cut.*

3. *In the four murders of which I have seen the notes only, I cannot form a very definite opinion as to the time that had elapsed between the murder and the discovering of the body.*

   In one case, that of Berners Street, the discovery appears to have been made immediately after the deed – In Bucks Row, Hanbury Street, and Mitre Square three or four hours only could have elapsed. In the Dorset Street case the body was lying on the bed at the time of my visit, 2 o'clock, quite naked and mutilated as in the annexed report – Rigor Mortis had set in, but increased during the progress of the examination. From this it is difficult to say with any degree of certainty the exact time that had elapsed since death as the period varies from 6 to 12 hours before rigidity sets in. The body was comparatively cold at 2 o'clock and the remains of a recently taken meal were found in the stomach and scattered about over the intestines. It is, therefore, pretty certain that the woman must have been dead about 12 hours and the partly digested food would indicate that death took place about 3 or 4 hours after the food was taken, so one or two o'clock in the morning would be the probable time of the murder.

4. *In all the cases there appears to be no evidence of struggling and the attacks were probably so sudden and made in such a position that the women could neither resist nor cry out. In the Dorset Street case the corner of the sheet to the right of*

the woman's head was much cut and saturated with blood, indicating that the face may have been covered with the sheet at the time of the attack.

5. In the four first cases the murderer must have attacked from the right side of the victim. In the Dorset Street case, he must have attacked from in front or from the left, as there would be no room for him between the wall and the part of the bed on which the woman was lying. Again, the blood had flowed down on the right side of the woman and spurted on to the wall.

6. The murderer would not necessarily be splashed or deluged with blood, but his hands and arms must have been covered and parts of his clothing must certainly have been smeared with blood.

7. The mutilations in each case excepting the Berners Street one were all of the same character and showed clearly that in all the murders, the object was mutilation.

8. In each case the mutilation was inflicted by a person who had no scientific nor anatomical knowledge. In my opinion he does not even possess the technical knowledge of a butcher or horse slaughterer or any person accustomed to cut up dead animals.

9. The instrument must have been a strong knife at least six inches long, very sharp, pointed at the top and about an inch in width. It may have been a clasp knife, a butcher's knife or a surgeon's knife. I think it was no doubt a straight knife.

10. The murderer must have been a man of physical strength and of great coolness and daring. There is no evidence that he had an accomplice. He must in my opinion be a man subject to periodical attacks of Homicidal and erotic mania. The

character of the mutilations indicate that the man may be in a condition sexually, that may be called satyriasis. It is of course possible that the Homicidal impulse may have developed from a revengeful or brooding condition of the mind, or that Religious Mania may have been the original disease, but I do not think either hypothesis is likely. The murderer in external appearance is quite likely to be a quiet inoffensive looking man probably middle-aged and neatly and respectably dressed. I think he must be in the habit of wearing a cloak or overcoat or he could hardly have escaped notice in the streets if the blood on his hands or clothes were visible.

11. *Assuming the murderer to be such a person as I have just described he would probably be solitary and eccentric in his habits, also he is most likely to be a man without regular occupation, but with some small income or pension. He is possibly living among respectable persons who have some knowledge of his character and habits and who may have grounds for suspicion that he is not quite right in his mind at times. Such persons would probably be unwilling to communicate suspicions to the Police for fear of trouble or notoriety, whereas if there were a prospect of reward it might overcome their scruples.*

I am, Dear Sir,
Yours faithfully,
Thos. Bond.'

Unfortunately, the authorities refused to take Bond's advice regarding the reward and the perpetrator was never caught. It is possible that he was arrested on an unrelated matter, committed to an asylum or even took his own life as the series of prostitute murders apparently ended with the Dorset Street slaying. The extent to which Mary Kelly was mutilated beyond all recognition suggests that the murderer's mind gave way – in clinical terms, his personality disintegrated under the internal pressure. In such a state he would not have been fit to be prosecuted.

Psychopathia Sexualis

Serial killers are not a modern phenomenon. In an earlier age, the savage mutilations carried out by what were known as lust murderers might have been attributed to vampires, werewolves and other malevolent creatures of the night by a superstitious community who could not bring themselves to believe that such acts could be committed by a fellow human being. Even when a human agent was identified as being responsible, as in the case of the Countess Bathory who bathed in the blood of young virgins and the child killer Gilles de Rais, those responsible were demonized by the church as servants of the Devil. The implication being that human beings could not have committed such acts unless possessed or corrupted by a malevolent godless entity.

It is a disturbing fact that contrary to popular belief, the crimes of Jack the Ripper were not unique. The mutilations which so horrified Victorian society were characteristic of a recognized mental disorder identified, diagnosed and recorded by the German-born psychoanalyst Richard von Krafft-Ebing almost a decade before the Whitechapel murders took place. Ebing's influential study of sexual aberrations, *Psychopathia Sexualis*, detailed numerous cases of sadistic sexual murder which bear a striking similarity to those perpetrated by the Ripper.

'It cannot be doubted,' observed Krafft-Ebing, 'that a great number of so-called lust murders depend upon a combination of excessive and perverted desire. As a result of this perverse colouring of the feelings, further acts of bestiality with the corpse may result – e.g. cutting it up and wallowing in the intestines.'

In referring to the Ripper murders in a later edition of the book its author noted, 'It is probable that he first cut the throats of his victims, then ripped open the abdomen and groped among the intestines. In some instances he cut off the genitals and carried them away; in others he only tore them to pieces and left them behind. He does not seem to have had sexual intercourse with his victims, but very likely the murderous act and subsequent mutilation of the corpse were equivalents for the sexual act.'

As for the authenticity of the 'Dear Boss' letters which were posted to the Central News Agency at the height of the terror and which gave rise to the notorious nickname by which the Ripper is remembered, former FBI profiler John Douglas dismissed them out of hand as did Metropolitan Police Commissioner Sir Charles Warren, who had been in charge of the original investigation. 'It's too organized, too indicative of intelligence and rational thought, and far too cutesy,' Douglas has said. 'An offender of this type would never think of his actions as funny little games or say that his knife's so nice and sharp.'

Profiling a Phantom

On the one hundredth anniversary of the Whitechapel Murders in 1988, two of the FBI's leading profilers, John Douglas and Roy Hazelwood, lent their extensive experience in tracking sexual predators and serial killers to the creation of a psychological profile of Jack the Ripper for a television special hosted by Peter Ustinov.

Considering the case solely on the facts as recorded in the official autopsy reports and Metropolitan Police files, they concluded that the Ripper was a white male in his mid to late 20s, of average intelligence whose success in evading detection was due simply to luck, rather than resourcefulness. His very ordinariness had enabled him to melt into the crowded courts, teeming streets and dark alleyways of the capital. Therefore, one could disregard the classic image of the slumming aristocrat in top hat and billowing cloak striding through the London fog and consider instead the likelihood that he was a local man, indistinguishable from his neighbours and unremarkable in his appearance.

There was, however, no apparent pattern to the murders; they were spontaneous, opportunistic slayings. Such predators always scour the same area starting near home and extending their killing ground as they grow in confidence. He may have felt compelled to return to the scene of his crimes to gloat or relive the frisson it had given him, a factor of aberrant behaviour that the police of the time would have been unaware of, otherwise they might have been able to keep an eye on the sites and catch him in the act.

According to Douglas and Hazelwood the choice of victim, together with the nature of the mutilations, indicates that the perpetrator might have been abused by a domineering female who had raised him and as a result he would have vented his rage by mutilating animals, bullying other children and eventually committing arson. These acts might have brought him to the attention of the police while he was in his youth and so he may have had a file that would have been worth looking into.

The fact that all the murders took place between midnight and 6 am indicates that the Ripper most probably lived alone and would have had few, if any, friends. He would have had a menial job, such as a slaughterman, that would have given him the opportunity to indulge his sadistic impulses undetected, and this occupation might also have provided the excuse he needed to be out and about during the early hours without arousing suspicion, even with blood on his clothes. It was not uncommon at the time to see slaughtermen in the streets and pubs of Spitalfields and Whitechapel in their blood-spattered aprons.

Armed with these details Douglas and Hazelwood felt confident in eliminating some of the prime suspects such as the Queen's physician Sir William Gull and Montague Druitt who drowned himself in the Thames shortly after the last murder. Having reconsidered the evidence they both agreed that the most likely suspect was a Polish vagrant, Aaron Kosminski, though Douglas has subsequently qualified his conclusion by saying the most likely suspect was someone like Kosminski.

From my own research I felt confident in ruling out Kosminski for the following reasons. Aaron Kosminski (1865–1919) was a passive imbecile who scavenged for scraps of food in the streets of Whitechapel and did not exhibit any form of violent behaviour at any time during his adult life. The strongest evidence against him was the belief that he had been committed to Colney Hatch asylum shortly after the murder of Mary Kelly, but even this is not true. He was actually committed in 1891 when doctors described him as apathetic. If he had been capable of committing murder, he would have been at liberty to do so for a full three years, from 1888 onwards.

Kosminski was a familiar figure in the East End and would have been recognized if he had been seen near the vicinity of the murder sites. Several witnesses had reported seeing a man of shabby genteel appearance which suggests a working man whose clothes had seen better days, whereas Kosminski was a dirty and dishevelled vagrant whom even the victims would have avoided. Furthermore, he didn't speak any English, whereas several witnesses claimed to have seen one of the victims shortly before their death talking to a man who does not appear to fit Kosminski's description and who was heard to speak softly in English.

In his place, I unearthed a previously unnamed suspect who fitted the profile and who was a similar type to Kosminski. My suspect was a butcher who lived in the heart of the Ripper's killing ground. He matched the physical description given by several key eyewitnesses and he had contracted syphilis from prostitutes for whom he was said to have a violent dislike. He too was eventually committed to an asylum and died in the year that Scotland Yard officially closed the case on the Whitechapel murders (see *The Crimes of Jack the Ripper*, Arcturus 2006).

The Vampire of Düsseldorf

'Tell me, after my head has been chopped off, will I still be able to hear, at least for a moment, the sound of my own blood gushing from the stump of my neck? That would be the pleasure to end all pleasures.'

Peter Kürten on the morning of his execution, 2 July 1932

When German psychoanalyst Dr Karl Berg entered Peter

Kürten's cell in Klingelputz prison shortly before his execution, he expected to be confronted by a gibbering lunatic, the wreckage of a man whose mind had given way to madness. As a frequent visitor to the *Irrenhaus* (mental asylum), Dr Berg had witnessed many disturbing scenes in his professional life, but the sight that greeted him that morning gave him cause to pause in the doorway. Kürten, a self-confessed butcher of more than 30 men, women and children, rose from his bunk, smoothed the creases of his tailored suit and presented himself to the Herr Doktor with a wan smile and the politeness of a provincial businessman with a proposition to discuss. It was an offer Dr Berg knew he could ill afford to refuse – the first in-depth, face-to-face interview in the history of crime between a serial murderer and a psychiatrist.

As Dr Berg composed himself, he wondered if the police were right to suspect that Kürten's confession might be no more than a sick fantasy. It seemed incredible that such a self-possessed, obsessively neat individual could be the sadistic monster the press had dubbed the 'Vampire of Düsseldorf'. But once the interview was under way, it was clear that the 48-year-old former factory worker was in deadly earnest.

The first thing that struck Dr Berg was Kürten's remarkable memory. He could recall each and every crime he had ever committed in vivid detail, all 79 of them, the emotional stimulation he derived from the act having seared them into his mind. Yet when it came to recounting mundane events in his life he proved as fallible as everyone else.

'It is very easy to describe crimes one has not committed,' Kürten patiently explained to his incredulous visitor. 'One could scarcely credit it that a confession could be founded on very full newspaper reports and yet be simply an invention. To that extent, I quite understand your doubts, Professor.'

Kürten blamed his sadistic impulses on his brutal father who had beaten his eight children with regularity, repeatedly forced himself upon their mother while they watched and committed incest with one of his own daughters before being arrested and imprisoned.

Despite Kürten's protestations of disgust he imitated his father's behaviour, raping his 13-year-old sister and torturing animals with the encouragement of the family lodger, a sexual degenerate who introduced Peter to the practice of bestiality. However, Kürten went one better than his mentor, stabbing the animals to death while he ejaculated.

If his testimony is to be believed, his first murder had occurred when he was just a boy. He drowned two school friends in the Rhine after one fell from a raft they were playing on and the other had dived in to save him. Peter held the second boy under the water, preventing him from rescuing the other.

The Crimes of Peter Kürten

Kürten's killing spree began on 25 May 1913 when he broke into a house in Müllheim near Cologne with the intention of stealing and was overcome by the urge to claim the life of a 10-year-old girl he found sleeping there. He throttled her until she was unconscious, then sexually abused her before slitting her throat with a pocket knife.

'I heard the blood spurt and drip on the mat beside the bed. It spurted in an arch, right over my hand. The whole thing lasted about three minutes. Then I locked the door again and went back home to Düsseldorf.'

Unfortunately, suspicion instantly fell on the girl's uncle Otto Klein, who had quarrelled violently the previous day with her father Peter over a loan. Otto had left in a rage threatening to do something which Peter would regret for the rest of his life. When the police found a handkerchief at the scene with the initials 'P.K.' on it they assumed that Otto had borrowed it from his brother and the case went to trial, but the handkerchief was considered insufficient evidence to convict him and Otto was freed.

Kürten revisited Müllheim the day after the murder where he found himself a seat in a café opposite the inn and gleefully soaked up the horror and indignation as the locals discussed the crime.

A lengthy prison sentence for arson and other offences kept Kürten off the street until 1921. When he emerged, he married and lived a respectable life for four years as a trade union representative. But in 1925 he returned to Düsseldorf to be greeted by what he perceived to be an omen. 'The sunset was blood-red on my return.'

For the next four years he contented himself with more arson attacks and burglaries, but on 3 February 1929 he again succumbed to his sadistic impulses, stabbing a woman 24 times before fleeing the scene. Had the police had the foresight to stake out the site, they might have caught Kürten and checked his reign of terror.

'The place where I attacked Frau Kühn I visited again that same evening twice and later several times. In doing so, I sometimes had an orgasm.' Four days later he murdered 8-year-old Rosa Ohliger, whom he stabbed 13 times before setting her body alight. There was no evidence of sexual assault, but Kürten had smeared semen inside the dead girl's underwear to degrade her and mark her as his own. 'When that morning I poured petrol over the child Ohliger and set fire to her, I had an orgasm at the height of the fire.'

Five days later he stabbed a 45-year-old mechanic to death and, true to form, returned to the scene the next day to chat casually with a policeman about the progress of the investigation.

Three people were repeatedly stabbed in separate incidents on 21 August after their attacker wished them good evening, then on the night of 23 August two young girls, aged 5 and 15, were strangled and decapitated at the Flehe annual fair.

The following afternoon, Gertrude Schulte, a domestic servant, was approached by a man answering to Kürten's description who repeatedly propositioned her. When she screamed that she'd rather die, he cried, 'Die then!' and plunged a knife into her. Incredibly she lived to give the police a good description of her assailant.

The list of attacks intensified during the following weeks with no sign that the killer was tiring of his work. Two young girls were raped and beaten to death and there were hammer attacks on two women at the end of October.

On 7 November, the body of a 5-year-old girl was discovered buried under rubble after her killer had sent a note and map (see opposite) describing where she could be found. Her body bore the marks of 35 knife wounds. That spring there were strangulations and more hammer attacks, but all the victims survived. The inconsistency in the madman's method and his ever-changing choice of weapons, however, misled the police into believing that they were looking for more than one man.

It was then that Kürten's conceit proved his undoing. On 14 May 1930, Maria Budlick, a domestic servant, was standing on

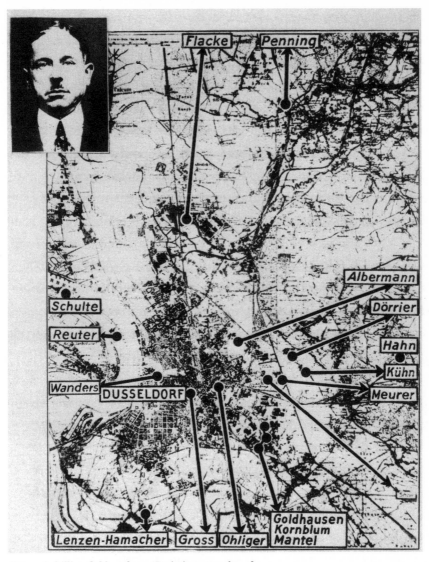

Kürten's killing fields, where 17 victims were found.

the platform at Düsseldorf station when a man approached her and offered to show her the way to the local women's hostel. She accepted his offer and they walked together into the city until he insisted they take a short cut through the park. It was then that she feared she might be in the company of the Düsseldorf Vampire and made an excuse to leave. But the man pressed himself upon her. At that moment a respectable gentleman appeared and offered his assistance. The first man left and Maria's gallant rescuer introduced himself. His name was Peter Kürten.

By this time Maria was hungry and tired, so she gladly accepted his cordial invitation to stay the night in his rooms, but when they arrived she changed her mind as soon as it became obvious that he expected her to sleep with him in return.

To her surprise he didn't insist but agreed to take her by tram to Worringerplatz where he would find her a cheap hotel. When they got off the tram, she must have felt she could trust him to keep his word as she allowed him to lead her into the Grafenberger Woods. Under the cover of the trees Kürten seized her round the throat and repeated his demand for intercourse.

> *'I thought that under the circumstances she would agree and my opinion was right. Afterwards I took her back to the tram, but I did not accompany her right to it because I was afraid she might inform the police officer who was standing there. I had no intention of killing Budlick as she had offered no resistance. I did not think that Budlick would be able to find her way back to my apartment in the rather obscure Mettmanner Strasse. So much the more was I surprised when on Wednesday, the 21st of May, I saw her again in my house.'*

This rather simple-minded servant girl had not only remembered his address but had written to a friend how she had been raped in the woods by a man living at that address. As fate would have it the letter was delivered in error to a woman with a similar name who on reading the contents immediately contacted the police. Kürten narrowly escaped arrest, but knew that the game was up. He made a full confession to his wife.

'Today, the 23rd, in the morning, I told my wife that I was also responsible for the Schulte affair, adding my usual remark that it would mean ten years or more separation for us – probably forever. At that, my wife was inconsolable. She spoke of unemployment, lack of means and starvation in old age. She raved that I should take my life, then she would do the same, since her future was completely without hope. Then, in the late afternoon, I told my wife that I could help her.' [His plan was for her to inform the police of his confession and claim the reward.]

'Of course, it wasn't easy for me to convince her that this ought not to be considered as treason, but that, on the contrary, she was doing a good deed to humanity as well as to justice. It was not until late in the evening that she promised to carry out my request, and also that she would not commit suicide. It was 11 o'clock when we separated. Back in my lodging, I went to bed and fell asleep at once.'

Kürten was arrested by armed police on 24 May 1930, outside St Rochus church. He went calmly into custody, assuring the police that they had no need to be afraid of him.

Kürten was formally charged with nine murders and seven attempted murders, but he subsequently confessed to 68 separate attacks. Many of these victims recovered from their wounds, but

Kürten boasted that there were still many more that would never be identified because no one would even know they were missing.

At his trial, which ran from 13 April 1931 to June 1932, he was caged behind an iron grille. In the courtroom an array of weapons was exhibited, including his knives, a hammer, a coil of rope and scissors alongside articles of his victims' torn and bloody clothes, several skulls and dismembered limbs recovered from their shallow graves.

The prosecution sat back and let Kürten condemn himself out of his own mouth in a long rambling monologue with which he criticized the authority of the expert witnesses and corrected inaccuracies in the evidence. There was little the defence could offer in response other than enter a plea of insanity, which was refuted by a number of eminent medical men who concurred that Kürten did not suffer from any known organic or functional mental disease and had been 'perfectly responsible for his actions at all times'.

As his lawyer remarked in despair, 'The man Kürten is a riddle to me. I can not solve it. The criminal Haarman only killed men, Landru and Grossman only women, but Peter killed men, women, children and animals; killed anything he found.'

The reason for his murder spree, Kürten claimed, was his desire to avenge himself on society for the wrongs it had inflicted upon him during the 24 years he had served in prison since his youth for petty offences such as thieving and arson.

'... So I said to myself in my youthful way, "You just wait, you pack of scoundrels!" That was more or less the kind of retaliation or revenge idea. For example, I kill someone who is innocent and

not responsible for the fact that I had been badly treated, but if there really is such a thing on this earth as compensating justice, then my tormentors must feel it, even if they do not know that I have done it ... I had to fulfil my mission.'

As a young man Kürten had resented prison life, but as he grew older, he eventually reconciled himself to long periods of incarceration and even welcomed them as an opportunity to indulge his sadistic daydreams. Occasionally, he would even provoke the guards into throwing him into solitary confinement, so that he could indulge his fantasies in the dark undisturbed by his fellow inmates. These included visions of mass murder with himself as the god-like mastermind overseeing the carnage.

'I thought of myself causing accidents affecting thousands of people and invented a number of crazy fantasies such as smashing bridges and boring holes in bridge piers. Then I spun a number of fantasies with regard to bacilli which I might be able to introduce into the drinking water and so cause a great calamity. I imagined myself using schools or orphanages for the purpose, where I could carry out murders by giving away chocolate samples containing arsenic which I could have obtained through housebreaking. I derived the sort of pleasure from these visions that other people would get from thinking about a naked woman.'

Kürten claimed he was driven to murder to relieve himself of tension and, as he recalled the killings in grisly detail, he exhibited all the signs of arousal, confirming Dr Berg's belief that his sadistic tendencies were sexual in origin. Stabbing was a sexual act, but it offered only a temporary release. Kürten's voracious sexual appetite could never be satisfied and sooner or later he would feel compelled to seek another victim. The obvious relish he derived from recounting his crimes led Dr Berg to conclude that Kürten was abnormal but not insane, while the obsessive pride he took in his appearance marked him out as a narcissistic personality who was so self-centred that he simply could not spare a thought for anyone else.

> *'I have no remorse. As to whether recollection of my deeds makes me feel ashamed, I will tell you. Thinking back to all the details is not at all unpleasant. I rather enjoy it … I committed my acts of arson for the same reasons – sadistic propensity. I got pleasure from the glow of the fire, the cries for help.'*

Perhaps the most puzzling aspect of Kürten's personality was his undying loyalty and concern for his wife, a former prostitute, whom he admired for her strength of character rather than her sensuality. Although he had shown no compassion for any of his victims and was habitually unfaithful, he surrendered to the police solely in order that his wife could claim the substantial reward.

> *'I had already finished with my life when I first knew the police were on my track. I wanted to fix up for my wife a carefree old age, for she is entitled to at least a part of the reward. That is why I entered a plea of guilty to all the crimes.'*

When asked if his conscience troubled him he answered flatly and candidly:

'I have none. Never have I felt any misgiving in my soul; never did I think to myself that what I did was bad, even though human society condemns it. My blood and the blood of my victims will be on the heads of my torturers. There must be a Higher Being who gave in the first place the first vital spark to life. That Higher Being would deem my actions good since I revenged injustice. The punishments I have suffered have destroyed all my feelings as a human being. That was why I had no pity for my victims.'

Kürten did not seek notoriety as many modern serial killers do, but sexual gratification. He was a pitiable and pathetic figure, more so because he assumed an air of dignity and sophistication he did not possess. He paid for his uncontrollable urges with his life, leaving Dr Berg the only person to profit from the affair. The professor's insights into the mind of a lust murderer enhanced his reputation and gave him a bestseller, *The Sadist*, which served as the basis for Fritz Lang's influential 1931 film *M*, starring Peter Lorre.

Chapter Two:
Mad, Bad and
Dangerous to Know

'All men would be tyrants if they could.'
Daniel Defoe

Psychological profiling is not practised exclusively by criminal investigators. In recent years it has been used increasingly by industry to determine an applicant's suitability for a senior post and also to determine an employee's fitness for work after a lengthy leave of absence due to stress-related illness. Shrewd political campaign managers have been turning to psychoanalysts for decades to assess the threat posed by rival candidates, and government agencies regularly seek the advice of behavioural psychologists to evaluate the strengths and weaknesses of potential enemies such as terrorist leaders and the heads of rogue states. One of the first and most penetrating profiles ever created was drawn up by American psychoanalyst Walter C. Langer for the United States Office of Strategic Services (OSS, which became the CIA) in the spring of 1943. His subject was the Nazi dictator

Adolf Hitler, whose brutal regime was threatening to plunge Europe into a new Dark Age.

The Great Dictator – Profiling Hitler

The report was commissioned by the head of the OSS, General William J. Donovan, who impressed upon Langer the importance of providing an in-depth psychological assessment of the Führer which could be used for propaganda purposes and perhaps even for determining future American military strategy.

> *'What we need is a realistic appraisal of the German situation. If Hitler is running the show, what kind of a person is he? What are his ambitions? How does he appear to the German people? What is he like with his associates? What is his background? And most of all, we want to know as much as possible about his psychological make-up, the things that make him tick. In addition, we ought to know what he might do if things begin to go against him ... Keep it brief and make it readable to the layman.'*
>
> The Mind of Adolf Hitler, Walter C. Langer,
> London: Secker and Warburg, 1973

Langer baulked at the thought that his assessment might influence allied strategic planning, but he knew that he was being offered a once-in-a-lifetime opportunity to probe the mind of a classic borderline personality in an unprecedented position of power.

Despite his many public appearances Hitler remained an enigma, worshipped by the German people as their saviour while being vilified by his enemies as the personification of evil. His intuitive military mind and shrewd political opportunism had made him master of Europe and shown that he was not the slavering, carpet-chewing clown depicted in Allied propaganda. Yet German émigrés and disaffected former followers had hinted that the former Austrian corporal was no Napoleon, but a volatile, unpredictable paranoid personality who fervently believed that Germany's fate was allied to his own. Such a man would make a fascinating study.

In the course of eight months' research, Langer and his assistants compiled 11,000 pages of material, including interviews with German exiles living in Canada and the United States who were known to have had direct contact with Hitler. This material was reviewed by three eminent psychoanalysts to ensure that no single analytical approach unduly influenced the conclusions.

The following extracts from this once Top Secret file offers

Langer characterized Hitler as 'a neurotic psychopath'.

not only a unique insight into one of the most confounding and impenetrable personalities of modern times, but also a significant example of the emerging science of criminal profiling.

As Langer was later to write:

'Psychoanalysis, alone, had devised a technique for exploring the deeper regions of the mind and exposing the importance of early experiences and unconscious components as determinants of personality development ... A survey of the raw material, in conjunction with our knowledge of Hitler's actions as reported in the news, was sufficient to convince us that he was, in all probability, a neurotic psychopath.'

Langer's opening remarks (below) might apply to any of the numerous serial killers and sociopaths who have come to public prominence in recent years and whom we are quick to demonize as evil.

'The world has come to know Adolf Hitler for his insatiable greed for power, his ruthlessness, cruelty and utter lack of feeling, his contempt for established institutions and his lack of moral restraints. In the course of relatively few years he has contrived to usurp such tremendous power that a few veiled threats, accusations or insinuations were sufficient to make the world tremble. In open defiance of treaties he occupied huge territories and conquered millions of people without even firing a shot. When the world became tired of being frightened and concluded that it was all a bluff, he initiated the most brutal and devastating war in history – a war which, for a time, threatened the complete destruction of

our civilization. Human life and human suffering seem to leave this individual completely untouched as he plunges along the course he believes he was predestined to take.

[Hitler is] generally regarded as a madman, if not inhuman. Such a conclusion, concerning the nature of our enemy, may be satisfactory from the point of view of the man in the street. It gives him a feeling of satisfaction to pigeon-hole an incomprehensible individual in one category or another. Having classified him in this way, he feels that the problem is completely solved. All we need to do is to eliminate the madman from the scene of activities, replace him with a sane individual, and the world will again return to a normal and peaceful state of affairs.

This naive view, however, is wholly inadequate for those who are delegated to conduct the war against Germany or for those who will be delegated to deal with the situation when the war is over. They cannot content themselves with simply regarding Hitler as a personal devil and condemning him to an Eternal Hell in order that the remainder of the world may live in peace and quiet. They will realize that the madness is not wholly the actions of a single individual but that a reciprocal relationship exists between the Führer and the people and that the madness of the one stimulates and flows into the other and vice versa. It was not only Hitler, the madman, who created German madness, but German madness which created Hitler. Having created him as its spokesman and leader, it has been carried along by his momentum, perhaps far beyond the point where it was originally prepared to go. Nevertheless, it continues to follow his lead in spite of the fact that it must be obvious to all intelligent people now that his path leads to inevitable destruction.

From a scientific point of view, therefore, we are forced to consider Hitler, the Führer, not as a personal devil, wicked as his actions and philosophy may be, but as the expression of a state of mind existing in millions of people, not only in Germany but, to a smaller degree, in all civilized countries. To remove Hitler may be a necessary first step, but it would not be the cure. It would be analogous to curing an ulcer without treating the underlying disease. If similar eruptions are to be prevented in the future, we cannot content ourselves with simply removing the overt manifestations of the disease. On the contrary, we must ferret out and seek to correct the underlying factors which produced the unwelcome phenomenon. We must discover the psychological streams which nourish this destructive state of mind in order that we may divert them into channels which will permit a further evolution of our form of civilization ... The problem of our study should be, then, not only whether Hitler is mad or not, but what influences in his development have made him what he is.'

Walter C. Langer, US OSS, 1943

Childhood Trauma

Langer identified Hitler's neurosis as having originated in his childhood. His father was a sadistic bully, and his mother had suffered several miscarriages before Adolf was born, and this led her to dote on him and fear for his health as he was a sickly child. The birth of a younger brother when Hitler was six years old created a rival for his mother's affections and prompted Adolf to fantasize about killing the new arrival. This is not an unusual reaction, according to Langer, but Adolf hated his brother with an intensity that was clearly abnormal. The child's premature death and Hitler's habit of brooding on the significance of the stillborn siblings led him to believe that his life was protected by Providence. This mutated into a messiah complex when he realized that his father was 23 years older than his mother. The pronounced age difference gave the young Adolf the idea that the hated brute might not be his real biological father and that he himself could be the product of an immaculate conception. The fact that Hitler was miraculously spared from the fatal illness that had claimed his younger brother and that his father later died after Hitler had repeatedly prayed for such an event would have reinforced this fantasy. But while these deaths ensured the rekindling of his mother's undivided attention, they brought with them a measure of guilt from having secretly desired the death of his father and brother which brought his mother such grief.

However, these factors in themselves cannot account for the unbalanced nature of Hitler's psyche. The primary factor was the volatile relationship between Hitler's overbearing, officious and brutal father and his over-indulgent, masochistic mother. When Hitler witnessed his hated father forcing himself upon the mother (which resulted in the birth of the younger brother), he felt betrayed by his mother and disgusted at his own impotence in not being able to defend her.

Hitler's subsequent neurosis took the form of a symptom known as 'transference' in which the subject unconsciously offloads their internal conflicts on to external objects or other individuals. According to Walter Langer, in Hitler's case, his father was externalized in symbolic form as the Führer's birthplace, Austria, his Fatherland, while his mother became symbolized by his adopted homeland, Germany. It is revealing that the German people have traditionally referred to their country as the Fatherland, but Hitler frequently referred to it as the Motherland.

Langer says, 'This transfer of affections was relatively easy inasmuch as Germany, like his mother, was young and vigorous and held promise of a great future under suitable circumstances. Furthermore, he felt shut off from Germany as he now felt shut off from his mother, even though he secretly wished to be with her. Germany became a symbol of his ideal mother and his sentiments are clearly expressed in his writings and speeches.'

Langer offered a few examples to illustrate Hitler's transfer of emotion:

'The longing grew stronger to go there [Germany] where since my early youth I had been drawn by secret wishes and secret love.'

And: 'I appeal to those who, severed from the Motherland, and who now in painful emotion long for the hour that will allow them to return to the arms of the beloved mother.'

Langer continued, 'Just as Germany was ideally suited to symbolize his mother, so was Austria ideally suited to symbolize his father. Like his father, Austria was old, exhausted and decaying from within. He therefore transferred all his unconscious hatred from his father to the Austrian state. He could now give vent to all his pent-up emotions without exposing himself to the dangers he believed he would have encountered had he expressed these same feelings towards the persons really involved.'

The Humiliation of Defeat

The outbreak of war in 1914 presented Hitler with an opportunity to satiate his thirst for violence which his volatile background had induced in him, but that was not the only reason he greeted the news of hostilities with unbridled enthusiasm. It offered an opportunity for him to reaffirm his masculinity which had been severely compromised by his unnatural obsession with his mother. This had resulted in an over-identification with the feminine aspect of his nature which Langer concluded may have made Hitler a passive homosexual.

Langer continued, 'We can now understand why Hitler fell on his knees and thanked God when the last war broke out. To him it did not mean simply a war, as such, but an opportunity of fighting for his symbolic mother – of proving his manhood and of being accepted by her. It was inevitable that he would seek enlistment in the German Army rather than in the Austrian Army and it was also inevitable, under these circumstances, that he would be a good and obedient soldier. Unconsciously it was as though he were a little boy who was playing the part of a man while his mother stood by and watched him. Her future welfare was his great concern and in order to prove his love he was willing, if need be, to sacrifice his own life for her.'

This also explains Hitler's powerless rage on learning of Germany's defeat at the end of the First World War, that he described as 'the rape of the Motherland'. Unable to accept the humiliation of defeat, he retreated inside himself by inducing a fit of psychosomatic blindness which the army doctors diagnosed as hysteria.

Hitler's virulent anti-Semitism is accounted for by the likely possibility that he was unconsciously assuaging his own guilt for his part in losing the war by laying the blame for Germany's capitulation at the door of the Jewish capitalists and communists who he accused of having stabbed Germany in the back.

This tendency to blame others for one's personal failings is typical of neurotic paranoid personalities. But Hitler was a mass of contradictions and complexes. No single category could account for all of his actions.

As Langer noted, Hitler's outstanding defence mechanism was one commonly called 'projection'. It is a technique by which the ego of an individual defends itself against unpleasant impulses, tendencies or characteristics by denying their existence in himself while he attributes them to others. From a psychological point of view, it is not too far-fetched to suppose that, as the perversion developed and became more disgusting to Hitler's ego, its demands were disowned and projected upon the Jew. By this process the Jew became a symbol of everything which Hitler hated in himself.

Sex and Suicide

The perversion to which Langer refers was Hitler's masochism, which expressed itself in his desire to wallow in self-loathing and filth. In the years following his mother's painful and protracted death from cancer, the young Adolf is thought to have slept in a Vienna doss-house with other homeless men and rarely washed or changed his clothes, despite the fact that he had the means to pay for a modest hotel room thanks to his father's civil service pension and an inheritance from an aunt.

In later life he suppressed this compulsion for the sake of his public image with the result that it erupted in a new form in private. It has been suggested that Hitler demanded that his mistresses urinate on him and it was this which drove several to attempt suicide.

Langer observed:

'In most patients suffering from this perversion the unconscious forces only get out of control to this degree when a fairly strong love relationship is established and sexuality makes decisive demands. In other cases where the love component is less strong the individual contents himself with less degrading activities. This is brought out clearly in the case of Rene Mueller who confided to her director, Zeissler, who had asked her what was troubling her after spending an evening at the Chancellory, "that the evening before she had been with Hitler and that she had been sure that he was going to have intercourse with her; that they had both undressed and were apparently getting ready for bed when Hitler fell on the floor and begged her to kick him. She demurred but he pleaded with her and condemned himself as unworthy, heaped all kinds of accusations on his own head and just grovelled around in an agonizing manner. The scene became intolerable to her and she finally acceded to his wishes and kicked him. This excited him greatly and he begged for more and more, always saying that it was even better than he deserved and that he was not worthy to be in the same room with her. As she continued to kick him he became more and more excited..." Rene Mueller committed suicide shortly after this experience. At this place it might be well to note that Eva Braun, his present female companion, has twice attempted suicide, [Hitler's niece] Geli was either murdered or committed suicide and Unity Mitford has attempted suicide. Rather an unusual record for a man who has had so few affairs with women.'

The Sanctuary as Symbol

According to Langer, it is evident that the Führer was still unconsciously seeking his mother's approval and protection when he built his Alpine mountain retreat at Berchtesgarten near Salzburg in the 1930s, as its structure could be seen as symbolic of a return to the womb. The French writer François-Poncet described a visit to the Eagle's Nest in *The French Yellow Book 1938–39* in terms which make the symbolism explicit:

'The approach is by a winding road about nine miles long, boldly cut out of the rock ... the road comes to an end in front of a long underground passage leading into the mountain, enclosed by a heavy double door of bronze. At the far end of the underground passage, a wide lift, panelled with sheets of copper, awaits the visitor. Through a vertical shaft of 330 feet cut right through the rock, it rises up to the level of the Chancellor's dwelling place. Here is reached the astonishing climax. The visitor finds himself in a strong and massive building containing a gallery with Roman pillars, an immense circular hall with windows all around ... It gives the impression of being suspended in space, an almost overhanging wall of bare rock rises up abruptly. The whole, bathed in the twilight of the autumn evening, is grandiose, wild, almost hallucinating. The visitor wonders whether he is awake or dreaming.'

Langer makes the point that, 'If one were asked to plan something which represented a return to the womb, one could not possibly surpass the Kehlstein or Eagle's Nest. It is also significant that

Hitler often retires to this strange place to await instructions concerning the course he is to pursue.'

Bitter and Twisted

In conclusion Langer observed:

'The foundations of all the diverse patterns we have been considering were laid during the first years of Hitler's life. Many of them, as we have seen, were due primarily to the peculiar structure of the home, while others developed from constitutional factors or false interpretations of events.

Hitler and Eva Braun in their fabulous mountain retreat.

Whatever their origins may have been, they did set up antisocial tendencies and tensions which disturbed the child to a high degree. From his earliest days, it would seem he must have felt that the world was a pretty bad place in which to live.

To him it must have seemed as though the world was filled with insurmountable hazards and obstacles which prevented him from obtaining adequate gratifications, and dangers which would menace his well-being if he attempted to obtain them in a direct manner.

The result was that an unusual amount of bitterness against the world and the people in it became generated for which he could find no suitable outlets.

... Most people are able to take the sting out of [the] fear of death through religious beliefs in life after death, or through the feeling that a part of them, at least, will continue to go on living in their children. In Hitler's case, both of these normal channels have been closed and he has been forced to seek immortality in a more direct form. He must arrange to go on living in the German people for at least a thousand years to come. In order to do this, he must oust Christ as a competitor and usurp his place in the lives of the German people.

The great danger is that if he feels that he cannot achieve immortality as the Great Redeemer he may seek it as the Great Destroyer ...

With him, as with many others of his type, it may well be a case of immortality of any kind at any price.'

Hitler's Henchmen

The Death Camp commandants who implemented Hitler's Final Solution with such ruthless efficiency considered themselves mere functionaries of the regime: bureaucrats whose defence was a collective *Nicht schuldig* (Not Guilty) on the grounds that they were merely following orders. Their wilful disregard for the suffering of their fellow human beings and their apparent ability to live a normal family life away from their murderous work gave rise to the term, 'the banality of evil'.

Franz Stangl (1908–1971) exemplified this sociopathic personality. As commandant of the Sobibor and Treblinka death camps it is thought that he supervised the extermination of around 900,000 innocent men, women and children and endorsed acts of brutality among countless more, which was to earn him a life sentence for crimes against humanity.

As superintendent of the Euthanasia Institute at Schloss Hartheim in the early years of the war, he had overseen the extermination of the mentally and physically handicapped who were deemed by the state to be unworthy of life. In 1942, having proven himself capable of implementing orders without question, he was appointed commandant of one of the most notorious extermination camps in occupied Poland, Sobibor (March 1942– September 1942) and later Treblinka (September 1942–August 1943) where he strutted among the emaciated inmates dressed in a starched white riding outfit.

By the end of the war he had amassed a considerable private fortune by stealing the last possessions of those he had hounded into the gas chambers, including 145 kilograms of gold and 4,000 carats in diamonds. Incredibly Stangl managed to evade detection

– despite a brief spell in prison in Linz after the war for unrelated offences – until he could be smuggled out of Germany through the so-called rat line to South America. It was not until 1961 that Austria finally submitted to international pressure and ordered his extradition, and another six years before he was arrested in Sao Paulo.

At his trial in 1970 he shrugged off the accusation that he had colluded in genocide by saying, 'My conscience is clear. I was simply doing my duty.' Stangl died of a heart attack in his cell on 28 June 1971.

During his incarceration he agreed to be interviewed by author Gitta Sereny, whose non-confrontational technique encouraged Stangl to reveal the degree of self-deception and denial which made it possible for him to live with the crimes he had committed.

During one particularly revealing meeting she asked him if it was true to say that he got used to the killings. He considered the question for a moment then admitted that he had. How long had it taken for him to become impervious to his victims' suffering, she wondered?

Months, he told her. 'It was months before I could look one of them in the eye. I repressed it all by trying to create a special place: gardens, new barracks, new kitchens, new everything; barbers, tailors, shoemakers, carpenters. There were hundreds of ways to take one's mind off it; I used them all.' He claimed that he had distracted himself by throwing himself into the administrative duties but it was not enough to erase the memories of what he had seen, and so he had taken a glass of brandy to bed each night in an effort to forget. But that image of the tortured martinet was at odds with the strutting, grinning figure in riding gear described by the surviving prisoners.

Had he ceased to think of the prisoners as human beings? Were they just bodies as far as he was concerned – with no distinction between the living, the dying and the dead?

One can't help but suspect that he had been preparing his answer for years in anticipation of the day his past would catch up with him.

'When I was on a trip once, years later in Brazil, my train stopped next to a slaughterhouse. The cattle in the pens hearing the noise of the train, trotted up to the fence and stared at the train. They were very close to my window, one crowding the other, looking at me through that fence. I thought then, "Look at this, this reminds me of Poland"; that's just how the people looked, trustingly, just before they went into the tins ... I couldn't eat tinned meat after that. Those big eyes which looked at me not knowing that in no time at all they'd all be dead.'

Unmoved, Gitta pressed her question once again. Had he ceased to think of the prisoners as human beings?

'"Cargo," he said tonelessly. "They were cargo ... I think it started the day I first saw the Totenlager in Treblinka. I remember Wirth standing there, next to the pits full of blue-black corpses. It had nothing to do with humanity, it couldn't have; it was a mass – a mass of rotting flesh. Wirth said, 'What shall we do with this garbage?' I think unconsciously that started me thinking of them as cargo."'

Even the fate of the children failed to move him. 'I rarely saw them as individuals. It was always a huge mass. I sometimes stood on the wall and saw them in the tube. But – how can I explain it – they were naked, packed together, running, being driven with whips like …' He didn't finish his thoughts.

Asked if he could not have stopped such atrocities, he feigned helplessness and laid the blame on the system and his superiors who had implemented it.

'"It worked," he confessed, "and because it worked, it was irreversible."'

Auschwitz, the grim conclusion to a culture of paranoia.

A forensic psychologist might not classify the petty bureaucrats of the Nazi regime such as Stangl, Rudolf Hoess, the commandant of Auschwitz, or even Adolf Eichmann, the architect of the Final Solution, as typical psychopaths, despite their complicity in mass murder and their endorsement of individual acts of unspeakable brutality. But these men were undeniably guilty of criminal acts on a scale unprecedented in modern times and were sufficiently intelligent to distinguish between right and wrong. The fact that they rationalized their behaviour by arguing that it was not their place to question superior orders reveals moral cowardice of the worst kind and that in itself is a form of pathology. They believed wholeheartedly in the Nazi ideology, specifically the principle that categorized Jews as *Untermenschen* (subhuman) and they put their personal ambition above all else in an effort to play a pivotal role in bringing Hitler's New World Order into being.

Stangl's insistence that he simply found himself in the wrong place at the wrong time and that anyone would have acted as he had done had they found themselves in the same situation is an indication of how deeply he was in denial. His habitual evasiveness is apparent in the many euphemisms he used in place of the word 'murder' and the lengths to which he went in order to deceive the inmates into believing that they were entering a resettlement camp.

At Sobibor, he had ordered the building of a fake train station to give the impression that the camp was not their final destination. He cultivated gardens to reinforce the lie that it was only a containment centre and he cynically ordered fake shower fixtures in the gas chambers. Clearly one does not have to bloody one's own hands to qualify as a murderer.

Face-Off – The Cuban Missile Crisis

During 13 days in September 1963, the world was poised on the brink of a third world war. The mental chess games of the Cold War had finally come to a climactic face-off between the USA and the Soviet Union following the discovery of secret Soviet missile bases just 90 miles (145 km) off the Florida coast on the Communist-controlled island of Cuba.

At first the Russians vigorously denied the existence of the weapons but were caught out in a lie when the American ambassador produced aerial photographs taken by a US spy plane at a critical meeting of the United Nations. While the military might of the two superpowers prepared for what they believed was the inevitable conflict, the heads of the two states, President John F. Kennedy and Premier Khrushchev, assessed the threat posed by the other and struggled to find a way to defuse the situation without losing face.

Khrushchev is believed to have consulted a psychological profile of Kennedy that had been prepared in August 1960 by Mikhail Smirnovsky, the Russian chargé d'affaires, in Washington, in the hope that it might provide a chink in the young president's armour.

In his memoirs (*Khrushchev Remembers: The Last Testament*, pp. 488–89) the Soviet Premier recalled, 'We had little knowledge of John Kennedy, [other than that he was] a young man, very promising and very rich – a millionaire ... distinguished by his intelligence, his education, and his political skill.'

Smirnovsky described Kennedy as a 'typical pragmatist', who would be flexible and willing to compromise if it served his own interests and that of his country, although he was also capable of keeping his true feelings and opinions close to his chest. His youthful energy would ensure he had the stamina to see a crisis through without flagging (Kennedy's chronic back problems were not public knowledge at the time), his position would be consistent and his acute, penetrating mind would ensure he grasped the essence of a situation and would not be distracted by non-essentials. Despite his youth and comparative inexperience, Kennedy was not to be underestimated. He was known to be cautious and exacting, waiting until he had all the facts before him before determining a course of action. He would be willing to negotiate with the Soviets but only from a position of strength and he had expressed his steely determination to hold on to West Berlin even if it heightened the risk of nuclear war.

'To Comrade N.S. Khrushchev
I send an analysis on Kennedy which is of interest, sent by the USSR Embassy in the USA (by charge d'affaires Comrade Smirnovsky)
A. Gromyko 3 August 1960
* * * * * *

JOHN FITZGERALD KENNEDY (John Fitzgerald Kennedy)
Political character sketch.
Kennedy's position on USA foreign policy issues.
  On issues of USA foreign policy and, above all, on the aspect of chief importance in foreign policy relations between the USA and the USSR, Kennedy's position, like his position on domestic policy in the USA, is quite contradictory.
  Kennedy views relations between the USA and USSR as

relations of constant struggle and rivalry, which, on different levels can, however, in his opinion, take on different concrete forms.

Considering that in the world there is a conflict of "basic national interests" of the USA and USSR and that because of this one cannot expect fundamental change in their relations, Kennedy nevertheless grants the possibility of a mutually acceptable settlement of these relations on the basis of a mutual effort to avoid nuclear war. For this reason Kennedy, in principle, advocates talks with the Soviet Union, rejecting as "too fatalistic" the opinion that "you can't trust" the Soviet Union, that it "doesn't observe treaties," etc. ...'

And on Kennedy as a person:

'He has, by all accounts, an acute, penetrating mind capable of quickly assimilating and analyzing the essence of a given phenomenon, but at the same time he lacks a certain breadth of perception, the ability to think over a matter philosophically and make appropriate generalizations. By the make-up of his mind he is more of a good catalyst and consumer of others' ideas and thoughts, not a creator of independent and original ideas.

In keeping with this Kennedy is very attached to the institution of advisors called upon to suggest interesting ideas and to work up detailed reports on various problems, but makes the final decision on serious problems himself, not entrusting this function to his underlings.

Kennedy understands people well and in general is a good organizer, as is evidenced, in particular, by the harmonious and *efficiently-running apparatus he has put together for his election campaign.*

Temperamentally, Kennedy is a rather restrained, dis-passionate, and reserved person, although he knows how to be sociable and even "charming" – it is this latter quality in particular which explains the popularity Kennedy gained in the primary elections in a series of states throughout the nation.

Kennedy is very cautious and avoids taking hasty, precipitous decisions, but does not display excessive indecision.'

We will never know how influential this profile was in determining Khrushchev's response to Kennedy. In the event, the crisis was averted when Kennedy out-manoeuvred the hawks in Khrushchev's cabinet by simply ignoring a demand to climb down and instead replied positively to an earlier conciliatory offer. Kennedy took the chance that the first communication had been a personal message from the Soviet leader who he assumed was as keen to avoid a destructive war as he was, while the more recent communication betrayed the tone of a belligerent committee suggesting that Khrushchev might have been deposed for having made the earlier offer. Kennedy gambled that Khrushchev was still in control and responded positively to the first message, offering to dismantle US bases in Turkey at a later date to help the Soviet leader claim that he had secured concessions and thereby restore his authority at home. The gamble paid off. The launch sites on Cuba were dismantled and the ships carrying the missiles returned to Russia.

More recently the US prepared psychological profiles of Saddam Hussein and Osama bin Laden to assess the threat posed by the Iraqi dictator and the al-Qaida leader, both of which demonstrate how close political and criminal profiling have become in our age of rogue states and fundamentalist terror cells.

Saddam Hussein – Palaces and Paranoia

Shortly before the first Iraq War in 1991, Dr Jerrold Post, a former psychiatrist for America's Central Intelligence Agency, was commissioned to provide a psychological assessment of the Iraqi dictator which the government thought could be useful in predicting his reaction to the threat of international political pressure or even invasion. As Walter Langer had done with Adolf Hitler 60 years earlier, Dr Post first identified significant themes in Saddam's life which he believed had shaped his character and fuelled his neurosis. The first was abandonment and abuse. Saddam's father died when his son was small, forcing his mother to entrust him to her brother, Khayrallah, who allegedly abused the boy. This combination of abandonment and abuse affected Saddam's psychological development, creating what psychologists call the 'wounded self', a victim who distrusts the world and everyone in it. His mother's remarriage did not repair the damage and Saddam left home at the age of eight to return willingly to his abusive uncle who nurtured the boy's fantasies of military glory.

Saddam's image of himself as a conqueror was shadowed by equally strong feelings of insecurity which were externalized in the palaces he was later to build for himself. The interiors were in the grand manner befitting a Persian potentate, while below ground, under the inlaid marble floors, was a bunker of reinforced steel and concrete housing communications equipment, an armoury and even an escape hatch for a helicopter. Both in real life and in his inner state Saddam was effectively under siege.

When besieged for real the wounded self is typically self-destructive. As with Hitler and other dictators, Saddam ordered the destruction of his own country's infrastructure and natural resources – the oilfields – to satisfy his vindictiveness. It is the typical, 'if I can't have it, no one will have it' response of the spoilt child.

'The Madman of the Middle East'

In December 1990 Dr Post warned the House Armed Services Committee against demonizing the dictator whom many in the West had called 'the madman of the Middle East'. Categorizing Saddam as 'crazy' suggested that he was unpredictable, irrational and impulsive, an assumption which was not borne out by his actions.

Cult of the leader: the many faces of Saddam Hussein.

On the contrary, the Iraqi leader was an ambitious and calculating political opportunist who could be as patient as a predator who waits for the right moment to strike. Psychologically he was sound, but politically speaking he was out of touch with reality. His world view was distorted and extremely limited. As with Hitler before him, the Iraqi dictator had convinced himself that his fate and that of his people were interdependent and he believed himself to have been singled out by fate to fulfil the role of their saviour.

Messianic Delusions

Dr Post was of the opinion that it was this belief in his messianic mission which convinced Saddam that he was not to be constrained by conscience, but could use violence against anyone who opposed him, for to oppose Saddam was to oppose the will of God. But aggression used in defence of an ideal invariably masks an underlying insecurity. Those individuals whose authority has been earned rarely feel the need to enforce it by pre-emptive strikes against their enemies.

Such acts of wilful, indiscriminate violence as Saddam demonstrated against the Kurds and against his political rivals reveal a strong streak of paranoia. Burning with self-righteous indignation, he ignored the fact that he created these threats and conspiracies, partly to unite his followers in the fight against a common enemy, but partly because he has a psychological need to be constantly at war, so that he would not have to face the real enemy within.

As with many such figures, the only way to ensure they back down when cornered is to give them a way to save face, as prestige and self-image are paramount. They have no inner resources or sense of self-worth.

Faced with a humiliating defeat such individuals would think little of unleashing their most fearsome weapons in an orgy of mass destruction rather than capitulate. Power is the only language dictators understand and the only enemy they will respect is one which demonstrates clarity of purpose and the resolution to see their struggle through to the bitter end. Wavering and prevarication are perceived as a sign of weakness.

> *'He will only withdraw from Kuwait if he believes he can survive with his power and his dignity intact.*
>
> *By the same token, he will only reverse his present course if his power and reputation are threatened. This requires a posture of strength, firmness and clarity of purpose by a unified civilized world, demonstrably willing to use force if necessary. The only language Saddam Hussein understands is the language of power.*
>
> *Saddam will not go down to the last flaming bunker if he has a way out, but he can be extremely dangerous and will stop at nothing if he is backed into a corner. If he believes his very survival as a world class political actor is threatened, Saddam can respond with unrestrained aggression, using whatever weapons and resources are at his disposal, in what would surely be a tragic and bloody final act.'*

Malignant Narcissism

Despite Dr Post's assertion that Saddam did not suffer from any known psychological disorder, many profilers and political psychologists would describe him as a classic example of malignant narcissism syndrome which is a comparatively common criminal type. The core components of this syndrome, as identified by psychoanalyst Otto Kernberg, are pathological narcissism, anti-social features, paranoid traits and unconstrained aggression. When such men attain positions of political power and influence, they will continue to pose a serious and sustained threat to neighbouring countries until deposed. According to leading political psychologist Aubrey Immelman, Research Director for the Unit for the Study of Personality in Politics in Minnesota, the core components of this syndrome manifest in the following ways:

1. Pathological narcissism

Saddam exhibits extreme grandiosity, over-confidence, and self-absorption to a degree that renders him incapable of empathizing with the pain and suffering of others. He is devoid of empathy and unmoved by human suffering, which permits him to commit atrocities against his own people as readily as he is willing to brutalize his enemies.

2. Anti-social features

The tenuous social conscience of malignant narcissists is governed primarily by self-interest. Malignantly narcissistic leaders like Saddam Hussein are driven by power motives and self-aggrandizement; however, their amorality permits them to exploit the principled beliefs and deeply held convictions of others (e.g. religious values or nationalistic fervour) to consolidate their own power. They are undeterred by the threat of punishment, which makes them singularly resistant to economic inducement, sanctions, or any other pressures short of force.

3. A paranoid outlook

Behind a grandiose facade, malignant narcissists harbour a siege mentality. They are insular, project their own hostilities on to others, and fail to recognize their own role in creating foes. These real or imagined enemies, in turn, are used to justify their own aggression against others.

4. Unconstrained aggression

Malignant narcissists are cold, ruthless, sadistic and cynically calculating, yet skilled at concealing their aggressive intent behind a public mask of civility or idealistic concern.

For all his aggressive posturing and threats of unleashing the Mother of All Battles, Saddam withdrew into his bunker when confronted with superior coalition forces during the first Gulf War in 1991, emerging only after his enemies halted on his border having fulfilled the UN mandate to liberate Kuwait. But when the US invaded Iraq in 2003, he watched his forces melt into the sands and reverted to the wounded self of his childhood, hiding in a hole in the ground where he was eventually found by US troops who took him into custody. Saddam was tried, found guilty of crimes against humanity and executed on 30 December 2006.

The Personality Profile of Osama bin Laden

In the wake of the September 11 terrorist attacks on New York and Washington, both the US intelligence community and the media were hungry for every morsel of information they could find on Osama bin Laden, the al-Qaida leader who had ordered the most devastating attack on American soil since Pearl Harbor. Political psychologist Aubrey Immelman presented one of the more serious psychological evaluations of bin Laden to the International Society of Political Psychology in Berlin in 2002, having studied the Saudi-born terrorist's background and analyzed his published opinions.

Immelman identified bin Laden as a puritanical compulsive (i.e. an extreme fundamentalist) whose characteristics are self-righteousness, the need to control others and the desire to demonstrate contempt for the materialistic world they despise by living a life of austerity and self-denial which they urge others to share. The support and adoration of their followers serves to confirm their warped world view. Such people justify their irrational resentment and anger by convincing themselves that the world is immoral and that they alone are righteous. Immelman told the ISPP, 'the world of puritanical compulsives is dichotomized into good and evil, saints and sinners – and they arrogate for themselves the role of saviour. They seek out common enemies in their relentless pursuit of mission. Puritanical compulsives are prone to vent their hostility through "sadistic displacements" and their puritanical wrath becomes the vengeful sword of righteousness, descended from heaven to lay waste to sin and iniquity ... [bin Laden's] kind of flaming righteousness is often rooted in a caring but controlling, virtuous but moralistic upbringing. Such child-rearing practices can breed adults who "displace anger and insecurity by seeking out some position of power that allows them to become a socially sanctioned superego for others."'

According to influential personality theorist Theodore Millon, puritanical compulsives like bin Laden are ambitious and

Bin Laden: an unprincipled narcissist?

exploitative, determined, dissenting, distrusting, dominant and dutiful to their cause. They accept leadership roles and expect others to recognize what they believe to be their unique qualities. They do not seek approval and act on the assumption that they have a right to do as they please. So-called Dauntless Individuals are forthright, courageous, persistent and uncompromising with little regard, or respect, for social laws or conventions. They habitually engage in high-risk activities with no regard for the safety of others and are manipulative and self-sufficient.

According to Immelman, bin Laden's personality patterns qualify him as one of Millon's 'unprincipled narcissists'.

This composite character complex combines the narcissist's arrogant sense of self-worth, exploitative indifference to the welfare of others, and grandiose expectation of special recognition with the antisocial personality's self-aggrandizement, deficient social conscience, and disregard for the rights of others.

Contrary to the public's image of the al-Qaida leader as a fanatical religious fundamentalist, it is Immelman's opinion that bin Laden does not fit the profile of the highly conscientious, closed-minded religious fundamentalist, nor that of the religious martyr who combines these qualities with devout, self-sacrificing features; rather, it suggests that bin Laden is adept at exploiting Islamic fundamentalism in the service of his own ambition and personal dreams of glory.

For ten years, bin Laden evaded detection and capture until May 2011 when he was finally traced to a house in a specially built compound close to the Pakistan Military Academy, 100 km (62 miles) from the capital Islamabad. He was killed there on the night of 2 May by a US special forces team of Navy SEALS and his body was disposed of at sea after a formal identification was made and photographs of the corpse were taken. It has been suggested that the compound had been built for him with the full knowledge of the Pakistan government and that the military academy had been established at the same time to provide protection from possible assassination or ground assault. It has been further alleged that a former senior Pakistan intelligence officer betrayed the world's most wanted fugitive for a $25 million reward after the al-Qaida leader had ensured his location could not be electronically traced through a mobile phone or internet connection. The Pakistan government denied all such allegations.

The Road to Terrorism

In the mid-1980s psychologist Eric D. Shaw devised what he termed The Personal Pathway Model, to describe the route by which terrorists are recruited. He identified its key stages as early socialization processes (meaning cultural conditioning and family circumstances); narcissistic injuries (wounds to the ego resulting in lower self-esteem); escalatory events, specifically negative experiences with authority; and a connection with a terrorist who becomes a role model or in the case of many women who join, a lover. Recruits may be inspired to join out of a warped sense of honour, to compensate for what they perceive as their family's failure to act on their beliefs or to stand up for perceived injustice.

If their parents had been devoutly religious or fervent nationalists, they may have condemned the use of violence. Their children, however, would have silently seethed at what they saw as their parents' impotence or unwillingness to fight back and so as soon as they attained the age when they could carry arms they would join a group in the belief that they carried the responsibility for restoring the family honour. It is for this reason that many highly educated individuals willingly sacrifice their future and their life for a cause. It is a myth that all terrorists are social misfits, although almost every cell has its uneducated outcasts (see page 72) who are motivated by a hatred of society in general. But no matter how righteous the cause might be in the mind of the terrorist and no matter how they seek to justify their violent acts against civilians, some psychologists believe that the desire to belong to a terrorist group is of itself symptomatic of an incomplete or fragmented psychosocial identity and violence will not solve that particular problem.

Terrorist Cells

'The outstanding common characteristic of terrorists is their normality.'

Martha Crenshaw, expert on terrorism, 1981

After the London suicide bombings of 7 July 2005, the Centre for Defence Studies at King's College and the Norwegian Defence Research Establishment organized a conference in the capital to thrash out ideas on how to combat the growing menace of terrorism in Europe. Among the assembled experts from around the world was Petter Nesser of the NDRE who had studied the background of the London suicide bombers and identified the four personality types who comprise a typical cell. He named these the entrepreneur, the protégé, the misfit and the drifter.

The leader of the 7 July cell, Mohammed Siddique Khan, fulfilled the role of entrepreneur because he was the activist who ensured the group's plans were put into effect. 'But this figure often needs contacts with a radical imam for religious guidance', Nesser remarked, 'and, for practical purposes, contacts with the jihadi infrastructure, though instructions can also be got from the internet.'

The second member of the group, Shezad Tanweer, exemplified the role of the protégé who considers the leader to be his mentor or surrogate older brother. He is typically well educated and would possess bomb-making and other practical skills that would be essential for any terror operation.

The third member of the cell, Hasib Hussain, embodied the third type known as the misfit. He was certainly not on a holy crusade, but simply searching desperately for something to belong to in order to give his unfulfilled life some meaning. He was a loser who was haunted by failure and burdened by problems which he believed would be solved by becoming part of a group who have come together for a specific purpose. He is also likely to be violent and unpredictable.

The fourth member of the London bombers was Jermain Lindsay, who would personify the fourth element of the typical cell, the drifter.

'This kind of person drifts into the group through circumstances or contacts,' explained Nesser. 'He might not have been an activist before and might not be entrusted with key details of the group's activities.'

Lone Wolves

'[There is] no such thing as an isolated terrorist — that's a mental case.'

Franco Ferracuti, criminologist

Not all terrorists operate within a cell. Richard Reid, the so-called shoe-bomber, worked alone and is what is known in counter-terrorist circles as a convert.

Alison Pargeter of King's College, London studied more than 30 converts and discovered that they shared very similar backgrounds. They were often psychologically and emotionally unstable individuals from impoverished or broken homes, an experience which had undermined their sense of security. This would make them vulnerable to recruitment by more extreme religious sects who would exploit their need for stability and acceptance. In effect the group would become their surrogate family.

However, not all of the experts are convinced that the answer to defeating extremists lies in profiling.

Dr John Horgan, a psychologist at the University of St Andrews, Scotland, argues that profiling cannot be applied to terrorists because they are not a homogenous population who can be identified and targeted and also because involvement in terrorism means different things to different people. There are many who sympathize with a cause but who do not become militants or activists and we simply do not know why some remain sympathetic but passive, while others act violently. Moreover, profiling of terrorists has been based on too small a sample and as everyone recognizes, there are untold numbers of radicals who will never engage in terrorist activity.

Dr Horgan told a reporter:

'The promise of being able to psychologically profile terrorists is beguiling. Risk assessments, however, considering a range of predisposing risk factors for vulnerability to radicalization, offer more useful alternatives. Involvement in terrorism is a complex process, and because of this, it is important to look at the ways in which a person gets drawn into terrorism from activities that have pretty mundane origins, and from that to develop tailored counter-terrorism strategies. There is an "IED" progression, from

involvement to engagement and then, in some, to disengagement from terrorism. At various points along these processes, we can identify vulnerabilities for controlling or influencing how a person moves into or out of one kind of activity or another.'

The Face of Terror

'There is no psychological evidence that terrorists are diagnosably psychopathic or otherwise clinically disturbed.'

Ken Heskin, psychologist, 1984

Two years before the al-Qaida attacks on New York and Washington, the American intelligence agencies and the Department of Defense were becoming increasingly concerned about the growing threat to political stability in the Middle East and elsewhere in the world posed by a multitude of terror organizations and guerrilla groups. In response the Federal Research Division of the US Library of Congress compiled the most comprehensive report ever published into the nature of terrorism and the factors which contribute to the making of a terrorist. Its author was Rex A. Hudson.

Under the heading 'The Process of Joining a Terrorist Group', Hudson noted:

'Individuals who become terrorists often are unemployed, socially alienated individuals who have dropped out of society. Those with little education, such as youths in Algerian ghettos or the Gaza Strip, may try to join a terrorist group out of boredom and a desire to have an action-packed adventure in pursuit of a cause

they regard as just. Some individuals may be motivated mainly by a desire to use their special skills, such as bomb-making. The more educated youths may be motivated more by genuine political or religious convictions. The person who becomes a terrorist in Western countries is generally both intellectual and idealistic. Usually, these disenchanted youths, both educated or uneducated, engage in occasional protest and dissidence. Potential terrorist group members often start out as sympathizers of the group. Recruits often come from support organizations, such as prisoner support groups or student activist groups. From sympathizer, one moves to passive supporter. Often, violent encounters with police or other security forces motivate an already socially alienated individual to join a terrorist group.'

The report goes on to state that these individuals are invariably highly motivated but their dedication to the cause is no guarantee that they will be accepted. Such groups tend to be security conscious to the point of paranoia. Their lives and liberty depend upon their identities being kept secret so they will not accept anyone who they believe will brag about their activities or betray their trust. They value recruits who are well educated and possess skills the group needs such as bomb-making or communications.

One of the most significant passages in the report questions the stereotypical image of the terrorist as a psychopath or fanatic with a political agenda. However, as several eminent psychologists have observed, psychopaths are a liability to the terror cell. They are indiscreet, unreliable, unpredictable and incapable of following orders. Cell members need to blend in with the local population and move about unobserved. But they do share a similar egocentric world view. Both personality types, the psychopath and the terrorist, see the world as comprising three groups of people: their idealized heroes, their enemies and the rest of society who they consider of no consequence.

Terror attacks require meticulous planning which is beyond the scope of unbalanced, disorganized individuals, although there have been exceptions. In April 1986 the Syrian-backed Jordanian Nezar Hindawi put his pregnant Irish girlfriend aboard an El Al flight to Israel, with the promise that he would follow as soon as he could so they could be married before the child was born. Fortunately for her and her fellow passengers, Heathrow airport security personnel discovered a bomb hidden in a false compartment of her hand luggage which Nezar had timed to explode when the plane was in mid-air.

Mentally unbalanced individuals have, however, been active in aeroplane hijacking.

The report cites a study carried out in 1971 by psychiatrist David G. Hubbard who concluded that the majority of plane hijackers were not terrorists but mentally disturbed individuals who sought to draw attention to themselves, not their cause. Since the 1970s airline hijackings have become a principal method of violent protest for terrorists, but still the majority of hijackings are carried out by disturbed individuals with no political agenda. We don't hear of these simply because they tend to occur on domestic flights and are usually resolved without loss of life and therefore receive little or no publicity. Hubbard's study revealed that these skyjackers were almost always passive neurotic underachievers who shared similar backgrounds, namely an alcoholic or violent father and an extremely religious mother.

Sins of the Fathers

'The urban guerrilla's aim is to attack the state's apparatus of control at certain points and put them out of action, to destroy the myth of the system's omnipresence and invulnerability.'

Baader-Meinhof communiqué

The belief that all terrorists are fanatics is as erroneous as stating that all killers are psychopaths. The members of the German revolutionary group the Baader-Meinhof Gang (aka the Red Army Faction) were a collective comprised of the children of former Nazis and their victims who wanted to punish a post-war society which had failed to bring their fathers or their father's murderers to account. According to the group, Germany was too eager to forgive and forget and had allowed former Nazis to infiltrate positions of power. As far as the group was concerned the state was still fascist in all but name and they would prove it by forcing the authorities to show their true colours.

'It wasn't just about killing Americans, and killing pigs, at least not at first,' wrote Richard Huffmann, author of the definitive history of the group, *The Gun Speaks*. 'It was about attacking the illegitimate state that these pawns served. It was about scraping the bucolic soil and exposing the fascist, Nazi-tainted bedrock that the modern West German state was propped upon. It was about war on the forces of reaction. It was about Revolution.'

The consensus of those who have studied the group in detail, such as psychologist Konrad Kellen and writer Gunther Wagenlehner, is that the members were not primarily political but were young student radicals suffering from a deep psychological

Andreas Baader during his trial.

trauma which led them to blame the government for their personal problems. Wagenlehner observed, 'These students became terrorists because they suffered from acute fear and from aggression and the masochistic desire to be pursued.' At the risk of sounding crass, they were playing cops and robbers with real guns. For them, terrorism was 'an individual form of liberation'. As with most terrorists the members of the group shared a common bond which in their case was alienation, but alienation is not a psychosis. A psychotic is motivated solely by self-interest and is incapable of learning from their experiences, whereas a terrorist is prepared to sacrifice themselves for the cause and often possesses the characteristics of a guerrilla fighter: resourcefulness, self-reliance and adaptability.

At the start of their campaign in 1971 the group could count on considerable support among German youth (a poll put it as high as 20 per cent). They were seen as rock star revolutionaries in their leather jackets and designer shades. Their choice of getaway car – the BMW 2002 – made the Bavarian sports car a fashion item for the affluent young German. But after their bombing campaign of May 1972 in which several US soldiers died, a judge's wife was crippled and dozens of innocent print workers were injured, the groundswell of support died away as Germans, young and old, considered themselves under siege.

Five weeks later, the leaders were all in jail. Four subsequently committed suicide and a fifth starved himself to death in prison. The revolution had failed.

Cult of Celebrity

A deprived childhood and physical abuse are not, of course, the only contributing factors in many cases of psychotic or aberrant behaviour. In modern society the pressure to succeed can put even the most well-adjusted adult under enormous stress. But if an individual has psychological or emotional problems the pressure to be somebody or nobody can have a detrimental effect on their mental state. Mark Chapman and John Hinckley Jr are just two examples of disturbed young men who turned their failure and frustration on the celebrities with whom they were obsessed. Beatles fan Chapman shot his hero, John Lennon, dead in New York in December 1980 in the belief that his name would forever be linked with the former Beatle. He had taken his obsession to an extreme, including dating Asian girls in imitation of Lennon's courtship of Yoko Ono, but there came a point when Chapman realized that the disparity between himself and his idol was simply too great to be narrowed by imitation. For Chapman, Lennon was not a person but the embodiment of everything he wished he could be, and so if he couldn't be Lennon, then no one could. Once Chapman had decided on his course of action, he became uncharacteristically calm, a sign that his inner struggle had found a resolution. But he had effectively programmed himself to carry out a mission, and so even after he had met Lennon outside the Dakota Building in New York and discovered that his hero was gracious he could not override it. He waited for Lennon to return and, when he emerged from his limousine, Chapman pumped five bullets into him. But even at that moment he claims all he could think about was how well the gun was working.

As for Hinckley, he attempted to assassinate US President Ronald Reagan as a gesture of devotion to his idol, screen star Jodie Foster, whom he had been convicted of stalking. Neither of these men killed, or attempted to kill, in anger, but were they legally insane, or merely obsessed?

Deadly Obsessions

'The movie isn't over yet.'
John Hinckley Jr

At Hinckley's trial the prosecution called on a number of psychiatrists to testify as to the defendant's mental state. They diagnosed the 26-year-old ne'er-do-well as suffering from three personality disorders: schizophrenia, narcissism and a blend of borderline passive-aggressive tendencies. He also exhibited symptoms of depression.

On the stand the prosecution's leading expert, Dr Park Dietz, quoted from a weighty 600-plus-page psychiatric report which had identified, 'a pattern of unstable interpersonal relationships; an identity disturbance manifested by uncertainty about several issues relating to identity, namely self-image and career choice; and chronic feelings of emptiness or boredom; features of passive-aggressive personality disorder include resistance to parental demands for adequate performance for occupational and social functioning, combined with dawdling ... inability to sustain consistent work behavior ... lack of self-confidence ...'

The press dubbed the disorder 'dementia suburbia', but it boiled down to shiftlessness. Hinckley was deceitful, work-shy and resentful of other people's success. He wanted fame and wealth, but was not prepared to struggle to get it.

'The desire not to work can be traced back at least to the time after Mr Hinckley's high-school graduation,' Dr Dietz claimed. 'I think that Mr Hinckley's interest in the Beatles is the earliest sign that I've been able to discern that he became exceedingly interested in fame, in the notion of success, in fame in a way that would not require a great deal of effort.'

Hinckley was determined to be famous at any cost and had an unhealthy interest in assassinations, but in clinical terms he was not insane. He knew the difference between right and wrong. Or as Dr Dietz put it, 'Mr Hinckley, as a result of mental disease or defect, did not lack substantial capacity to appreciate the wrongfulness of his conduct.'

Prior to his assassination attempt on Reagan on 30 March 1981, Hinckley had carefully considered the effects of different bullets and had worked out how to obtain the best shot. He had analyzed the security situation surrounding the president and on the day in question had waited for the most opportune moment to fire. If he had been insane, he would have acted on impulse, blazing away wildly unaware of anyone else. The fact that he waited until the security detail were looking away from him indicates that he knew what he was doing was wrong.

But the defence were determined to put a spin on the old saying by proving that there are lies, damn lies and expert opinions. They put their own psychiatric expert on the stand, Dr David Bear, to testify that Hinckley was psychotic on the day he attempted to kill the president. It was necessary to prove his incapacity if he was to avoid a lengthy jail term. After interviewing Hinckley, Bear had concluded that he exhibited classic symptoms of schizophrenia and clinical depression, but the most revealing remark he had made was when he told the doctor he had a mission to rescue Jodie Foster from Yale University where she was studying during a sabbatical from acting. 'Every single time a psychiatrist sees thinking like that,' said Bear, 'every time, not as a matter of opinion, as a matter of fact, that is psychosis.'

Dr Bear refuted the prosecution's claim that Hinckley may have been faking psychosis by saying that frauds tend to say they have seen visions or have been hearing voices directing them to do evil acts, whereas Hinckley exhibited subtle but significant symptoms such as failing to react to questions which should have elicited an emotive response.

In support of their argument the defence attempted to introduce a CAT-scan of Hinckley's brain which they claimed proved his mental disorder had a physical origin. After much legal wrangling, the judge ruled that the scan could be admitted as evidence, the first time this form of medical evidence had been allowed in an American court. According to Dr Bear, the photo of Hinckley's brain revealed widened sulci (folds and ridges) on the surface which are a common feature in the brain of schizophrenics.

John Hinckley Jr poses for an image that was used in evidence at his trial.

After a long deliberation, the jury returned a unanimous verdict of not guilty by reason of insanity. Public outrage was reflected in the subsequent highly charged press coverage that demanded the law be changed to prevent violent criminals from seeking sanctuary in the insanity defence. As a result of the protests, several states redefined their statutes, others decreed that the burden of proof was to be moved from the prosecution to the defence, while yet others acted to restrict the testimony given by psychiatric experts to specific issues. Three states abolished the insanity defence altogether.

Chapter Three:
The FBI Files

'You feel the last bit of breath leaving their body. You're looking into their eyes. A person in that situation is God!'

Ted Bundy, serial killer

New York is no stranger to terrorism. Long before the terrorist attacks of 9/11 the city was effectively under siege from within by a faceless figure the press had named 'the mad bomber'. Between the late 1940s and the mid-1950s several of the Big Apple's most celebrated landmarks including Grand Central Station and Radio City Music Hall had been targeted by the anonymous fanatic, who had placed more than 30 bombs in public buildings as part of a seemingly motiveless hate campaign. The bomber didn't demand a ransom to cease his activities. And this was one of the factors that intrigued Greenwich Village psychiatrist Dr James A. Brussel, to whom the police turned in 1957 in their desperation to identify the perpetrator.

Profiling
Dr Brussel effectively invented modern offender profiling as he examined the crime scene photographs and studied the bomber's

taunting letters to the press. From these he concluded the suspect was a paranoiac who hated his father, was obsessed by his mother and was or had been an employee of Consolidated Edison, a public utility power company to whom the majority of the letters were addressed. Other details revealed that he was likely to be suffering from a heart condition and lived in Connecticut. Dr Brussel concluded his report with the prophetic words, 'Look for a heavy man. Middle-aged. Foreign-born. Roman Catholic. Single. Lives with a brother or sister. Chances are when you find him he'll be wearing a double-breasted suit. Buttoned.'

Brussel dismissed what was to prove to be an uncannily accurate description as the result of mere deductive reasoning and his considerable experience as a psychiatrist. He was confident in stating that the suspect was middle-aged because paranoia takes up to ten years to develop and the first bomb had been planted in 1940. Therefore, if the cause of the condition had occurred around 1930, the suspect would have to be in his 40s or 50s by 1956. As for the man's fastidious appearance, that was a safe assumption because one of the symptoms of paranoia is that those suffering from the complex often hold a grudge for years before they act on it and are obsessively neat. They also consider themselves intellectually superior to others and will manifest this in their appearance. The wording of the letters revealed that the individual was educated, but the absence of slang pointed to an outsider rather than a native New Yorker and the phrase 'dastardly deeds' hinted at a foreigner. Bombs were the favoured weapon of Central Europeans, while his imposing build was simply an educated guess. A German study had thrown up the intriguing fact that 85 per cent of paranoiacs are heavily built. As for the suspect being single, Brussel deduced this from the exaggerated curve with which he accented the letter 'w', suggestive of female breasts, revealing an individual who is sexually repressed.

The physical description would fit too many men in the state for the FBI to have investigated each individually, but Brussel suggested a way to flush their man out into the open. To exploit his simmering resentment against whoever he considered had wronged him, the newspapers should print an open letter offering a forum for his grievances, which being a paranoiac he would need to have acknowledged. Within days, three letters arrived at the newspaper office all criticizing Consolidated Edison for exploiting their employees; one even let slip the date of the incident that had outraged the author, 5 September 1931.

Armed with this information investigators trawled through the personnel files of Con Ed, looking for a past or present employee with a grudge dating back to autumn 1931. It wasn't long before

James Brussel, drink in hand, with colleagues during a murder trial.

they came upon the name of George Metesky who had filed a claim for compensation as the result of an injury at work, but whose request had been rejected on the grounds that it was not as debilitating as he had stated. Metesky fitted the profile like a glove. He was a heavy-set, 54-year-old, Polish-born Roman Catholic suffering from a heart condition. He lived in Waterbury, Connecticut with his two unmarried sisters and when detectives arrived at the house in the early hours of 21 January 1957 and invited him to the local police station for questioning he changed into a buttoned, double-breasted suit for his long-anticipated public appearance, just as Dr Brussel had predicted.

When asked to account for his uncanny accuracy, Dr Brussel answered that he had simply reversed the technique he used when diagnosing his psychiatric patients. Instead of examining the subjects' behaviour in order to predict how they might respond under certain conditions, he had been able to pin down the type of personality the police were looking for by studying his actions. This process is known as inductive reasoning (making qualified assumptions based on experience) and is the basis of behavioural science, as opposed to forensic science which is based on deduction (i.e. coming to conclusions from a logical analysis of known facts).

Pioneers of Profiling

If credit is to be given to any one individual for seeing the potential use of behavioural profiling in the field of law enforcement it must be Howard Teten, who had paid his dues with the California Police Department before joining the FBI in 1962. By 1969 the softly spoken, 6 ft 4 in (1.93 m) ex-US marine, who looked every inch the distinguished college professor in his wire-rimmed glasses, took the initiative to teach National Academy recruits a course he called Applied Criminology, which he later changed to Applied Criminal Psychology, the foundation of modern profiling. He sought out Dr Brussel in New York and asked the psychiatrist to teach him everything he knew. Brussel is said to have told Teten he couldn't afford his fees, but as it was for the public good he would share his insights into the criminal mind for free. Brussel must have been a remarkable teacher because, when Teten returned from New York, he was able to crack numerous unsolved cases by offering uncannily accurate profiles of the offenders to his former students, most of whom were serving police officers from out of state.

One of Teten's earliest successes resulted from an inquiry by an officer from his old beat in California. A woman had been stabbed to death by a killer who had left no forensic evidence or physical clues of any kind. Teten advised the officer to knock on doors in the victim's neighbourhood looking for an unattractive, scrawny loner in his late teens who would be wracked with guilt and bursting to confess. 'If a nervous-looking youth answers the door,' Teten told the officer, 'just stare him down and tell him, "You know why I'm here."' Sure enough, two days later the cop called to say that he had called on apartments in the area where the body had been found, but when a youth answering the description saw the policeman on his doorstep, he didn't get a chance to say his line before the kid blurted out, 'Okay, you've got me!'

G-Men

During the 1970s, the FBI's Applied Criminal Psychology courses were largely being taught by young academy graduates with no direct experience of the crimes they were describing. When they took their lectures on the road to instruct regional police departments in the new techniques they would often find their version of events being contradicted by a detective who had actually worked on that particular case. That and the fact that seasoned law enforcement officers often resented being taught by 30-year-old graduates seriously undermined the Bureau's efforts to make the case for behavioural science as an invaluable new weapon in the fight against crime.

Matters were not helped by the fact that the Bureau has not always treated profiling and the other soft sciences such as hostage negotiation techniques and even sex crimes with the seriousness they deserved. The National Academy's classroom courses were largely theoretical and very basic. Contemporary Police Problems, for example, covered such arid topics as community relations and the Sociology class offered little more than would be taught on a college psychology course. Even the sex crimes classes were more entertaining than informative with aberrant behaviour presented as eccentric rather than potentially dangerous. Credit for the development of a more cerebral approach to law enforcement must be given to individual agents such as Pat Mullany, Bob Ressler, Dick Ault, John Douglas, Roy Hazelwood and Howard Teten, who pursued their own informal programme on the quiet during the last years of the Hoover administration. The Director was, by all accounts, a despotic disciplinarian who demanded that his men – almost all of whom were white – should model themselves on Hollywood's G-Men ('Government Men', slang for the FBI), tracking down public enemies to their lairs rather than sitting behind their desks getting fat between the ears. Hoover was said to harbour a paranoid distrust of women, insisting that there should be no female personnel in the Bureau other than secretaries and filing clerks. And he made a point of having all graduates warned of the dangers of communist 'honey traps', alluring female spies allegedly planted in US cities to seduce FBI agents into betraying their country.

Ambitious agents, or blue-flamers as they were known in the organization, who were keen to make a favourable impression, were advised by their supervisors to write an ingratiating letter to Mr Hoover in the hope of receiving an autographed photo of the Director to pin on their office wall, but even these eager agents were actively encouraged to get out of the office by their supervisors and catch their quota of criminals, as if they were travelling salesmen on commission. Consequently many were forced to pass their time at the local library or go window shopping until called in to assist in an active investigation.

Inevitably, the more self-motivated graduates became frustrated with this Bureaucratic mentality and initiated their own, unofficial studies into criminal behaviour. Special Agent John Douglas, a genial 6 ft 2 in (1.88 m) former college football player whose later experiences provided the background for Thomas Harris's *Silence of the Lambs*, engaged offenders he had just apprehended in casual conversation while they sat in the back of a police car waiting for the patrolmen to finish taking witness statements. From these informal interviews, Douglas learned that habitual criminals invariably choose their way of life because it fulfils a need. As one professional gambler admitted, he would always find something to bet on even if it was only which of two raindrops on a pane of glass would reach the bottom first. 'You can't stop us, John,' he told the agent, 'no matter what you do. It's what we are.'

It was this simple statement that set Douglas on the path to becoming the first full-time profiler in the FBI.

Bank robbers proved to be a rich source of material. After questioning a number of them over a period of months, Douglas began to identify a common pattern of behaviour and, having done this, he was then able to instigate proactive strategies to catch them in the act.

How to Rob a Bank

It is common knowledge among law-enforcement professionals that criminals rarely rob banks during the working week. Every self-respecting thief knows that on Friday afternoons the vaults will be bulging with workers' wages and that it simply is not worth their while risking their liberty for anything less than the big weekly pay-out. But what the police and the FBI didn't know until the late 1970s was how criminals chose which bank to hit.

John Douglas, head of the FBI's Investigative Support Unit.

During his informal chats with bank robbers, Douglas learned that all professional thieves practised a form of profiling. They sized up their target, whether this was a potential victim or a bank, and assessed the risk against the likely reward. For many career criminals, part of the buzz of robbing or breaking and entering a premises was knowing that there was a chance of being caught as well as being able to get away with it. Many took a professional pride in their ability and audacity. They made sure that they did their research thoroughly before the big day. Some chose banks that provided quick escape routes such as those on busy main roads or just off the interstate highways. Others preferred small provincial banks in remote rural locations where there were likely to be few witnesses and enough distance from the nearest police station to guarantee a clean getaway. Banks with only female employees offered a comparatively soft target and, if a bank had no windows on to the street, that would put it at the top of their list. If there were no windows overlooking the street, they wouldn't be seen in the act by passers-by and the bank employees wouldn't have a chance of catching sight of the getaway car.

Criminals are commonly thought of as only one rung up the evolutionary scale from Neanderthals, but Douglas discovered that many put as much time and thought into assessing the risks as the average businessman. The trouble was that the banks were rarely as conscientious. Provincial branches and independent banks could be unbelievably lax when it came to security. They would routinely forget to renew the film in their surveillance cameras, or neglect to reset a silent alarm after an employee had tripped it accidentally. Such incidents were so common in certain towns that the local police would often take their time to respond, thinking that it was yet another false alarm. After the robbery these banks would return to their normal state of affairs as if they had just dealt with a difficult customer. They had learnt nothing. But the robber improved his technique with every heist because his liberty and his income depended upon not being caught. Often he would come back a few months later to see if any improvements had been made and, if not, he might take a second crack at it.

Armed with this knowledge the police would instruct the banks how to improve their security and make these improvements highly visible. But they would leave one vulnerable bank in each town to act as bait. With their options narrowed, the unsuspecting thieves would be forced to hit the one unsecured bank where armed officers in plain clothes would be posing as customers and tellers ready to arrest them.

Douglas was crucial in introducing a simple system of codes to frustrate the robber whose MO involved grabbing the manager as he arrived to open up in the morning and waiting with the hostage for each employee to walk in and be captured in turn. All the manager had to do when he arrived was turn on a light, or move a plant in the window to signal that all was well. If the first employee arrived and didn't see whatever pre-arranged signal had been agreed upon, they were to alert the police.

Tellers were also trained to drop the hold-up note behind the counter to preserve a potentially significant item of evidence. And they were to note the ID or licence plate belonging to any customers who routinely asked for non-essential services, such as small change or information on opening an account on the chance that they might be casing the branch for a future robbery.

Bonnie and Clyde pose for the camera in 1932.

Predictably, the bank robbery clear-up rates went into record figures. Small town banks are no longer a soft option and successful robberies in Europe and the US are now extremely rare. Having said that, the argument can be made that when one door closes the enterprising criminal finds that another one opens and the brighter bank robbers might have moved into internet fraud or any other form of easy income. But the days of armed robbery in our high streets are all but over.

Hostage-Takers

In the 1970s, hostage negotiation situations offered the Bureau's future profilers some of their most instructive on-the-job training. In the wake of the 1972 Munich massacre, there had been several audacious aeroplane hijacks in Europe and the Middle East by Palestinian terrorists who had succeeded in publicizing their cause before blowing up the empty planes and evading justice by fleeing to a friendly Arab country. Such exploits inevitably gave every armed robber and political extremist in Europe and the US the idea that they too could seize hostages if their plans went awry, then secure safe passage across the border. At the time the authorities had no guidelines on how to defuse these situations and no techniques for establishing a rapport with these individuals, who they saw only as desperate and unpredictable. Without adequate training, many liquor store hold-ups and thwarted bank robberies turned into the kind of media circus portrayed in the Al Pacino film *Dog Day Afternoon* which was based on a real robbery that had taken place in New York. But America wasn't the only country where hostage negotiation was inadequate at that time. In 1973 an attempted bank robbery in Stockholm had been frustrated by the Swedish police, who allowed the situation to drag on for so long that the hostages eventually came to identify with their captors and even assisted them against the police, a condition which became known as Stockholm Syndrome. Clearly, the authorities had to devise an official strategy for dealing with increasing incidents of this nature. In their criminology classes FBI trainees were limited to listening to recordings of real-life hostage scenarios and debating what they would do in a similar situation. Their mentality was fossilized in the Hoover era, with teachers asking their students to imagine how they would deal with a child molester or murderer who had taken hostages, which these types of offender rarely do. They did not even have the benefit of role playing to appreciate the criminal's point of view until it was introduced in the 1980s.

A typical teaching case used an incident that had occurred in St Louis in the late 1970s which the FBI used as an example of how not to handle a hostage situation. A camera captures the moment a young black man attempts to hold up a bar which is then surrounded by the police. Instead of bringing in a trained negotiator to establish a relationship with the offender and find out what his demands are, the police officers take turns trying to persuade him to surrender. As the tension mounts, several can be heard talking at once and, worst of all, patronizing him and jive talking rather than offering him a way out together with a guarantee that he will be treated fairly if he calms down and listens to reason. Whenever the gunman does try to seek reassurance that he won't be shot the minute he steps outside, the officers continually interrupt him. By the time the chief of police arrives, the gunman is highly distressed and the last thing he needs is to be told officially that his demands will not even be listened to until he releases all his hostages. Backed into a corner, he turns the weapon on himself and the camera captures the moment he puts a bullet in his own brain.

In contrast to the confusion which characterized that incident, profiler Pat Mullany managed to defuse a similar situation around the same time in which a mentally disturbed black male had held a senior police officer and his civilian secretary hostage at Warrensville Heights police headquarters in Ohio and demanded that all white men should leave the planet immediately. The gunman, Corey Moore, was a diagnosed paranoid schizophrenic and unpredictable in the extreme. After the TV cameras surrounded the building and the siege was shown on the daily news, President Jimmy Carter offered to speak with Corey in an effort to resolve the situation. It is always a bad move to offer a hostage-taker direct access to a decision-maker. The one thing that cannot be risked in a volatile situation like that one is having someone who can say 'no', because that can leave the gunman with no option but to start shooting or risk losing face. The trick is to keep them talking, wear down their resistance over time and appeal to their reason, or at least show that you share their desire to bring the crisis to a conclusion. Delaying tactics can only be utilized when there is an indistinct chain of command, so that the negotiator can pass on the demands without being put in the position of making promises they can't keep, or having to say no. Besides, if every fanatic or cornered gunman believes he is going to be given the chance to air his grievances to the president, the governor or the mayor, incidents of this kind will occur with increasing frequency and every hoodlum will demand it before they even consider surrendering. Mullany gave Moore a sympathetic hearing despite his ludicrous demands and promised him a press conference in which he could air his views, which secured the release of the hostages without a shot being fired.

Subtle Signals

A shrewd and experienced negotiator can profile a hostage-taker during the course of their conversations and spot significant clues in their language and attitude which can help end the crisis peacefully. Moore's impossible demands were clearly an expression of his mental illness, but negotiators have since learnt that when an otherwise rational individual suddenly ups the ante by making an impractical demand he is signalling that he realizes that the game is up and is thinking ahead to his trial, or even further. In the early 1970s aeroplane hijacker Gary Trapnell, a white offender, demanded the release of a black political activist, although he had never shown any interest in politics. The police assumed it was a stunt to draw the attention of the TV cameras that were camped out on the runway, but it later transpired that Trapnell knew he didn't have a chance of escape and was gambling that his support for the activist would curry favour with the black convicts he was going to be sharing a shower with.

Taking the BS Out of Behavioural Science

By the end of the 1970s profiling was being practised on an ad hoc basis by an informal collective of FBI agents based at the National Academy at Quantico, Virginia, but it had yet to be established as a serious branch of forensic science. The term itself was still unknown even to those who worked in the Behavioral Science Unit based in a windowless bunker 60 ft (18 m) underground, beneath the main teaching block.

When John Douglas took over as chief of the Behavioral Science Investigative Support Unit in 1986, one of the first things he did was to change its name to the Investigative Support Unit and, when asked why, he would reply that he wanted to take the BS out of Behavioral Science.

The Serial Killer – Facts and Fiction

'We all go a little mad sometimes.'

Ted Bundy, quoting Norman Bates in *Psycho*

Hannibal 'The Cannibal' Lecter (notably portrayed by Anthony Hopkins in *The Silence of the Lambs*) has wormed himself into the public consciousness as the personification of the urbane, softly spoken and strangely seductive serial killer: the antithesis of the wild-eyed wackos and greasy, fat, middle-aged, mother-fixated men we imagine living in their dingy basements surrounded by human remains.

But the unsettling fact is that neither image is realistic and that the true face of the serial killer generated by forensic profilers is more likely to resemble your neighbour, work colleague or even your partner.

Alfred Hitchcock's slasher classic *Psycho* gave birth to the idea that all serial killers live with their widowed mothers. In fact they are far more likely to live alone because they are sociopaths who can only mimic compassion for others and are therefore unable to sustain meaningful relationships. However, some may live with what forensic psychologists call a nurturing female who may be attracted to their dependency and veneer of vulnerability. Criminals of all types are habitually manipulative, but sexual predators and serial killers are particularly adept at conning victims into giving them what they want (which includes their nurturing female).

Movies and TV crime series are largely to blame for depicting serial killers as highly intelligent individuals who enjoy playing sophisticated mind games with the authorities. In real life, the majority of criminals spend their day in mundane activities avoiding detection until the urge to kill overcomes their natural caution. They only stop if they are caught or become physically unable to engage in what is both a physically and emotionally strenuous activity. The act of murder is an exhausting business and if it involves having to dispose of a body the effort can leave the perpetrator physically and emotionally drained for days. Killers who can boast the highest body count have invariably accumulated that amount of victims because they have been cautious and kill infrequently. Only fictional characters indulge in killing sprees and have any expectation of remaining at liberty.

The most successful serial killers (i.e. those who evade capture for most of their criminal career) rarely demonstrate cunning or a pre-planned strategy. They tend to be opportunists who attack lone females or children in an isolated place and kill them by strangulation, stabbing or slitting their throats as they need to demonstrate their physical superiority over their victims. Those who shoot their victims usually do so because it's a convenient method of silencing a victim they have raped or tortured.

It is rare for a serial killer to keep newspaper clippings of their crimes or a drawer full of souvenirs. Even the most compulsive and obsessive know that personal items can prove their connection to the victim. In many cases they prefer to revisit the murder site or linger in the crowd while the police investigate the scene. Their

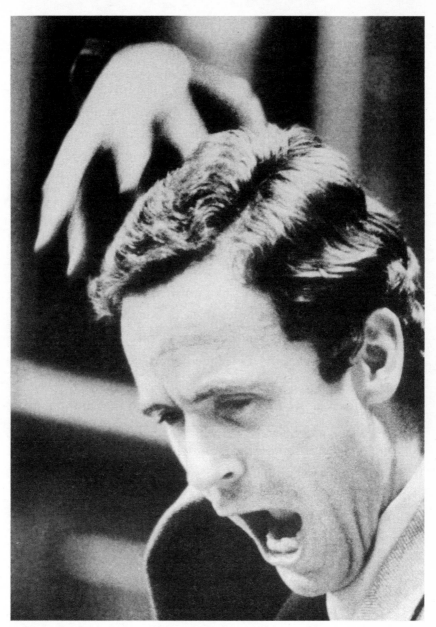

Ted Bundy reacts to news of his death sentence.

inflated sense of self-importance and eagerness to follow the case may even compel them to volunteer to join the search party or offer a witness statement.

The only hard fact that can be singled out from the mythology is that almost all serial killers come from dysfunctional backgrounds and the vast majority are men, almost all of whom will have suffered abuse of one kind or another in their formative years. It is thought that males are predominant because most violent murders are either sexually motivated or the result of a perverted male–female power struggle. Some speculate that it may be to do with male testosterone levels or masculine mental processes. Female serial killers are in the minority because women generally internalize anger. They tend to punish themselves with drugs, alcohol, self-destructive relationships or suicide. Those who kill are more likely to victimize their own children or those in their care, whereas male offenders frequently target strangers.

The FBI estimate that at any one time there are upwards of 50 serial killers active in the United States and that they could be responsible for as many as 6,000 slayings every year. Fortunately, most offenders are caught through their own carelessness, either from clues left at the scene of an earlier crime when they were relatively inexperienced and thus less cautious, or through their own over-confidence at the tail end of their career.

Contrary to the picture painted by Hollywood and procedural TV crime series, the biggest contributing factor to their capture is good old-fashioned luck.

Psychodrama

After investigating the crimes of Ted Bundy and dozens of

other serial killers, homicide detective Robert Keppel came to the conclusion that these individuals were not committing an unrelated series of killings but were acting out different scenes in a single psychodrama. Each murder involved the same characters, featured identical dialogue, repeated the same plot and came to the same sickening end, but the drama itself was evolving and if one knew the story one could stop the killer from playing it out.

Fortunately, many signature killers become increasingly addicted to their compulsion to the point where they lose control over their mental processes, become careless and neglect to clear away clues that ultimately lead to their capture. This process is known as 'devolving'. In layman's terms they go to pieces under the relentless pressure exacted on their minds and emotions by their obsessive repetitive behaviour. Their minds give way completely to the rage they have allowed to surge up from their troubled subconscious.

This process is common for signature killers from Jack the Ripper (whose final victim was mutilated beyond recognition) to David Berkowitz, the 'Son of Sam' whose taunting letters to the police displayed a progressive degeneration in his handwriting and a marked increase in grammatical errors.

The Art of Murder

FBI profilers have a saying, 'if you want to know the artist, study his art', meaning that for many signature killers murder is their only means of self-expression. If you want to know what is inside their head, you have to look at what they did to their victims. Another method is to talk to them, face to face, preferably in prison after their appeal has been turned down so they will have less reason to withhold information or to lie. After all, who better to talk to about what goes through a murderer's mind than the offender himself? And that is the conclusion John Douglas and his partner Bob Ressler came to one day in early 1978 after the monotonous routine of teaching criminal psychology from second-hand sources had led them to a dead end. It was one of those ideas which seem so simple that one wonders why no one had thought of it before, but the simple fact is that they hadn't. By implementing what was to become the first of several serious studies into the mind of serial offenders, Douglas, Ressler and their fellow FBI agents took the emerging science of criminal profiling out of the classroom and in a radical new direction.

Douglas counted on the fact that the majority of criminals like

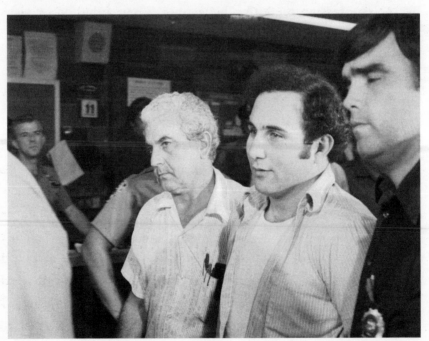

David Berkowitz, a 24-year-old postal worker, turned out to be the 'Son of Sam'.

nothing better than talking about themselves and basking in the recognition they imagine their crimes had earned them. From dawn to dusk each and every day of their sentence these men had nothing better to do than think about themselves, to crow about how they had outwitted the authorities and brood on the mistakes they had made that eventually led to their capture. Douglas and Ressler expected that a few genuinely remorseful individuals might welcome the opportunity to unburden themselves, but the majority would probably co-operate because they would relish the chance to share their fantasies with those they imagined would appreciate their art. Of course, there is an inherent danger in relying on self-reporting when conducting any form of research and especially one which involves convicted felons who habitually elaborate. But as long as their stories would be independently verified and the subjects could be interviewed in prison with no risk and no cost to the state there was everything to be learnt and nothing to be lost.

Wary of Bureau interference, Douglas and Ressler decided to conduct their initial interviews informally without official approval. So, whenever they had a few hours to spare after a road school seminar, mainly at evenings and weekends, they would check out the local penitentiary and see who was in residence. The pair thought that the best approach would be to arrive at the prison unannounced even if it meant there was a chance their chosen subject might refuse to meet them and make it a wasted trip. Their thinking was that if they made an appointment word might spread that an inmate was going to be talking to the FBI and someone would be sure to jump to the wrong conclusion. It also gave their chosen subject no time to talk themselves out of it and they wouldn't feel the need to have their attorney present which would seriously cramp the agents' style and impose restrictions on what topics could be discussed. The object was to get these guys to open up in a way they had never done before, not even to the cops to whom they initially confessed, nor to their attorneys, their shrinks or their social workers. Only the prison warden would know of the visit in advance.

Face to Face

Entering a maximum security penitentiary was as intimidating for the federal agents as it must have been for any convicted felon on his first day inside. Agents eat and sleep with their standard issue Smith and Wesson .38 revolver and even take their weapons with them to the bathroom, so for Douglas, Ressler and their colleague John Conway to surrender their guns at the gate of the California State Medical Facility at Vacaville where they had arranged their first encounter would have left them feeling naked and vulnerable. But even more unnerving was having to sign a waiver absolving the prison authorities of responsibility in the event they were taken hostage, as every state has a policy of refusing to negotiate with inmates, even for the lives of law enforcement personnel.

It was under these circumstances that the agents came face to face with the first interviewee on their shortlist, multiple murderer Ed Kemper, a disarmingly amiable giant just three inches shy of seven feet (2.06 m) tall and weighing an imposing 300 pounds. Even Douglas – a former athlete and a healthy height himself – was intimidated by the figure that stood before him dressed in prison work clothes, his black hair sleeked back, a broad moustache and thick-rimmed glasses giving him the look of the prison janitor. It was Kemper's build and awkwardness which had got him into trouble in the first place. The neighbourhood kids in Burbank had figured him for an oddball and picked on him mercilessly, especially once they knew he wouldn't fight back. Ed's mother only added to his troubles. She got it into her head that her son would rape his own sister if he had the chance, so she locked him up every night in the windowless basement which terrified him, and instilled a hatred for his mother that festered inside him for years. Even his daylight hours had been hell as his parents argued bitterly and violently until they finally separated while Ed was still at an impressionable age. He then went to live with his grandparents on their farm in the Sierras until the day his grandmother insisted he help her with the household chores. He shot her, then stabbed her repeatedly with a kitchen knife. When his grandfather returned from the fields he shot him too. It was August 1963 and Ed Kemper was 15 years old. He was confined to a mental institution where he remained until 1969 when he was released into the care of his mother against the advice of the state psychiatrists who considered him extremely dangerous. In this case they were right.

Over the following few years Ed roamed the Santa Cruz highways picking up pretty female hitchhikers and college girls, all of whom he murdered as mechanically as if he was wringing the neck of a chicken. Then he would have sex with their dead bodies before dissecting and decapitating them.

As he explained it: 'If I killed them, you know, they couldn't reject me as a man. It was more or less making a doll out of a human being ... and carrying out my fantasies with a doll, a living human doll.'

Ed Kemper arrives in court to be arraigned on eight counts of murder.

On 14 September 1972, Ed attended a formal interview with the California state psychiatric board who were to evaluate his progress with a view to sealing his juvenile record. Ed may have been seriously disturbed, but he wasn't stupid.

He knew exactly what the doctors wanted to hear and he had no intention of giving up his freedom. He gave a convincing performance as a truly contrite and reformed character and was duly declared no longer a threat to himself or to others. As he drove away, he must have been mighty pleased with himself for in the boot was the head of his latest victim, a 15-year-old schoolgirl.

Other killings followed over the next 18 months, all credited to the man the media had dubbed the 'Coed Killer'. Female college students in Santa Cruz were warned not to accept lifts from strangers, but Ed's mother worked at the college and had a college sticker on the windscreen of her car with which he used to pick up his victims. The presence of the sticker and Ed's laid-back act led the girls to set aside their reservations and accept his offer of a lift. He then killed them, taking the body back to his mother's house where he had sex with the corpse before carving them up in the bathtub and disposing of the parts in the surrounding hills or in the ocean at Carmel. He was clearly deranged and sick by anybody's definition, but his sense of irony remained as sharp as ever. In January 1973, he buried the head of one victim face up in the backyard looking towards his mother's bedroom because, as he told his interrogators later, she'd always wanted people to look up to her.

But by March that year, strangers no longer satisfied him. For years he had stolen into his mother's bedroom while she slept and imagined what it would feel like to crack her skull like an eggshell and watch the life 'seeping out of her'. One night over the Easter weekend, he tired of this fantasy, crept into her room and did it for real. He bashed her skull in with a claw hammer, then decapitated her and raped the headless corpse. In a final act of defiance he cut out her voice box and stuffed it down the garbage disposal in the kitchen sink. 'It seemed appropriate,' he later confessed to the police, 'she'd bitched and screamed and yelled at me over so many years.' But the disposal spat it back at him. 'Even when she was dead, she was still bitching at me! I couldn't get her to shut up!'

But Ed wasn't done yet. He then invited one of his mother's friends over for a surprise dinner and, when she arrived, he battered and strangled her before cutting off her head. Then he dragged the body in his own bed and went to sleep in his mother's bed as if nothing untoward had occurred. The next morning he took her car and drove eastwards fully expecting to be the subject of a state-wide manhunt, but there were no flashing blue lights in the rear-view mirror, no screaming sirens in the distance and nothing on the radio about a deranged killer on the loose. Frustrated and bitterly disappointed, Ed pulled over and made a call from a public phone box to the police offering to turn himself in. Perhaps not surprisingly they took a good deal of convincing before they finally sent out a patrol car to pick him up.

Douglas and Ressler were familiar with the facts long before they visited Kemper in prison. In fact, they used his case as a teaching tool at the Academy, but they had never seen the monster up close and personal. When their initial shock at being confronted by a man of his enormous stature had passed, they found themselves warming to his affable demeanour, his frankness in speaking of the appalling crimes he had committed and his obvious intelligence.

Kemper had a proven IQ of 145, way beyond that required to join the police. He was curious to know about the study they were conducting and showed a keen analytical mind when it came to categorizing his own disorders, bolstering the widely held belief that many of the acknowledged experts on the criminal mind are to be found behind bars. However, Kemper showed no remorse. The only subject that put a crack in his composure was when he recalled the abuse he had suffered at his mother's hands.

It was difficult for the agents to keep in mind that this rather disarming individual was by anyone's definition seriously disturbed, and was still considered by the prison authorities to be extremely dangerous. They only realized how close they were to a real monster when the guard was slow to arrive to take Ed back to his cell. While they waited, Ed reminded them that they were unarmed and that if he wanted to, he could twist off their heads and set them on the table between them before the guard could be summoned to subdue him. And what was to prevent him from doing so? He was in for life. The prestige he would gain from the other inmates for killing two FBI agents with his bare hands would be a fitting climax to his criminal career. The agents couldn't be sure he wasn't winding them up. How could he be certain they were not carrying concealed weapons, they asked him? Ed seemed to pause for a moment weighing up the risk; or was he just enjoying another sick joke? A moment later the guard appeared and unlocked the door. The interview was over.

Rogues' Gallery

Over the following months the team managed to interview half a dozen serial killers, including David Berkowitz, the self-named

'Son of Sam' who had shot courting couples in their cars, and Jerome Brudos whose shoe fetish became so all-consuming that it led him to kill four women and cut off their feet, which he kept in his freezer, to complete his extensive collection of ladies' footwear. From Berkowitz the agents learned that serial murder is often the last stage in a continuum that begins with cruelty to animals and can escalate into arson, which is an extreme expression of sexual frustration, although it may not appear as such on the surface. For many arsonists fire is a fetish, something that provides them with sexual excitement and satisfaction. Berkowitz gleefully admitted in his interview with the agents that he would stand in the crowd and watch the drama he had created while bringing himself to a climax. Before he graduated to murder he had set more than 2,000 fires in Brooklyn and Queens, all of which were described in his diaries with the obsessive attention to detail characteristic of a trainspotter, including particulars of the equipment and even the weather conditions on the night of the blaze. Many of the incidents were small nuisance fires started in trash cans and abandoned buildings to draw out the fire engines, but inevitably this was not enough and he graduated to murder. Armed with this knowledge Douglas advised police to instruct their crime scene photographers to take pictures of the crowd at every suspicious blaze. If they saw a guy with a transfixed look on his face and a hand down his trousers they would ask him to step aside and answer a few questions. Chances are that he would be their arsonist.

In addition the agents interviewed several would-be assassins, walking the gauntlet through the crowd of lifers milling around the exercise yard at Baltimore City Penitentiary to meet Arthur

Bremer who had failed to assassinate Governor George Wallace and enduring abuse from two of Charles Manson's deranged groupies who had attempted to prematurely end the presidency of Nixon's successor, Gerald Ford.

The Dark Guru

They also came face to face with the diminutive mad messiah himself, still sporting the scars from the swastika he had scored into his forehead with a razor blade during his trial. The dark guru of the Summer of Love was doing life at San Quentin for instigating the murder of Roman Polanski's pregnant wife, Sharon Tate, and a number of other innocent Californian citizens. When Douglas and Ressler met him in a small conference room off the main cell block, he was still protesting his innocence in a strained, overwrought voice accompanied by nervous animated gesticulations like a cartoon character on speed. He hadn't actually killed anyone personally, he told them, his wild hypnotic eyes darting from man to man. The state had convicted him of casting a spell over his followers and needed a scapegoat for all that had gone wrong with society. At least that was the gist of his interminable, rambling monologue which the agents were forced to endure. There was no need for them to have worried how they would get him to talk. The problem was getting him to talk about what they wanted to know. So they allowed him to climb on a table and address them from on high, knowing it would pander to his inflated ego to talk down to them, lecturing them on the hypocrisy of capitalism and the corruption endemic in the American judicial system. Patience and persistence were two of the prerequisites for the prisoner interview programme and both were tested to the limit by characters like Manson. Fortunately, they only had to pander to his paranoia for a few hours. It could be worse. They could have been sharing a cell with him. But for all his fortune cookie philosophy and twisted logic, Manson opened the agents' eyes to the dynamics of mind control exerted by the leaders of dangerous cults such as the Branch Davidians under David Koresh, who they were to deal with at Waco and elsewhere in the coming decades. Manson told them that he had singled out lost souls he knew he could dominate and then by telling them what they wanted to hear, that pollution was poisoning the planet and to make love not war, that they would begin to believe in him. So when he asked them to do something against the law their moral centre would be confused. During this indoctrination he would use sleep deprivation, starvation and psychedelic drugs to break down their resistance and make them totally dependent upon him, all the while telling them that these deprivations were spiritual disciplines designed to make them stronger.

Other subjects were less charismatic but no less delusional, leaving Douglas to conclude that many violent criminals were prey to conflicting emotions and these were at two extremes of the spectrum. They knew they were losers and had failed to measure up to what their parents or guardians had expected of them so they overcompensated by displays of feigned superiority and acts that demonstrated their contempt for society and its laws.

Their self-image was a delusion, but the stress of living a lie could not be sustained for long without periodic relief. Initially, masturbatory fantasies would be enough, but in time they would feel compelled to act on them in order to reinforce the illusion that they were in control.

Charles Manson with self-inflicted swastika.

As for the would-be assassins, they were compensating for their perceived inferiority by attempting to associate themselves with somebody who had achieved something in life. They tended to be paranoid and would avoid eye contact. All of them had kept a diary of some kind which effectively helped them to psych themselves up for the grand gesture that would bring them the recognition that they so desperately sought. By assassinating a leading politician, preferably a president, these nobodies would become somebody, if only by association. If they claimed to be acting for a cause, it would be an emotional overlay to justify their action, an excuse with which they could justify murder in their own mind. The other common factor was background. All violent offenders were the product of dysfunctional families and the majority had suffered abuse or neglect. Berkowitz, for example, was illegitimate and had been told by his adoptive parents that his mother had died in childbirth. He grew up blaming himself for her death. But later he discovered that she was still alive and decided to visit her. It was a disaster. She didn't want to know him and it traumatized him. But as Douglas and Ressler observed, many other people have suffered similar experiences and manage to cope. An abusive childhood is no excuse for inflicting pain on others. 'We can argue whether or not we are responsible for what we are, but in the overwhelming majority of cases we are certainly responsible for what we do.' (Douglas)

The Thousand-Yard Stare

During this time the agents perfected their interviewing techniques and became more astute at reading their subjects. They dressed down to put the inmates at their ease and spent hours in small talk to allow the prisoners to go through their act, repeating the lies they had fed their lawyers, the prosecutors, the jury, the prison psychiatrists and themselves. Once they had their say and felt sufficiently sorry for themselves they would open up, reliving their crimes in grisly detail and that is when Douglas became aware of what he called the thousand-yard stare. Whenever interviewees described their crimes, a glazed look would come into their eyes and they would look into the middle distance as if that moment was being replayed like a movie in a corner of the room. That is when the agents knew they were finally getting the truth.

Conclusions on Criminality

The first series of informal interviews raised sufficient interest in law enforcement circles for a second, larger and more scientifically rigorous study to be commissioned and funded by the National Institute of Justice focusing exclusively on 36 violent sex offenders. This landmark study was to be supervised by Dr Ann Burgess, professor of psychiatric nursing at the University of Pennsylvania, who helped compile a 57-page questionnaire to be filled out by the agents after each interview. At the end of this Douglas felt that he still hadn't had a definitive answer to the question which plagues everyone who tries to understand criminal behaviour – namely, are criminals born or are they made? However, there appeared to be compelling anecdotal evidence to suggest that certain individuals had a predisposition to violent behaviour which their background and early childhood experiences had exacerbated. If they also lacked a positive paternal role model and had poor impulse control they would not be psychologically fit to cope with the abuse they suffered and so would retreat into fantasies in which they externalized their anger. If these issues were not addressed their resentment could ultimately boil over and determine their actions. A supplemental question remained though, whether these offenders would have had the same murderous fantasies if they had benefited from a stable home life or constructive intervention. But even if they had, in Douglas' opinion they would most certainly not have acted on them and that insight alone justified the project. The key concept here is what is known as the feedback filter. A youth who is caught shoplifting and given a lecture on right and wrong by a caring adult whom the boy respects will be shocked back on to the straight and narrow. But a youth who perceives his actions as having increased his credibility with his peers and who derives a stimulating buzz from the attention he has attracted has learnt how to find fulfilment and will intensify his efforts and refine his technique, ensuring that he limits the risk of being caught.

Although 81 per cent of the offenders admitted to using pornography on a regular basis Douglas was emphatic that even the most extreme material would not turn normal men into sexual predators. However, sadistic pornography would inflame men who were already obsessed with such things and may give them specific ideas with which to develop their fantasies.

While the theoretical points raised by the study would be argued over for years, its practical applications were obvious and could be put into force almost immediately. New categories of offender were identified (see Organized vs Disorganized Offenders, page 131) and significant insights were gained into how crime scenes could be staged (see page 142) and what could be learnt from the location and condition of the victim, all of which helped to shape the processes and procedures that would determine the development of profiling.

Conning A Conman

Although all of the subjects in the original FBI research project were violent criminals, other categories of offender were questioned in a subsequent series of interviews. In the late 1980s Agent Gregg McCrary coaxed and cajoled forger and bomber Mark Hofmann into speaking for the first time at length about his crimes. Hofmann had faked nearly 500 religious artefacts for the perverse pleasure it gave him to fool the Mormon Church and the gullible art collectors he despised, then killed two innocent people with home-made pipe bombs in an attempt to divert attention away from his activities. A third detonated prematurely in his car, injuring him and bringing the whole affair to the attention of the federal authorities. McCrary considered it a personal challenge to convince the infamously uncommunicative and unrepentant con into opening up and had devised a strategy that played on his innate narcissism. McCrary prepared himself thoroughly for the interview by reading two biographies of the man experts were calling one of the greatest forgers of all time, as well as a thick file of cuttings on the case. He came to the conclusion that his subject was a highly educated and intelligent psychopath who would be wary of confiding anything to the authorities. He would only co-operate if he believed it would be in his best interests to do so. Conmen of Hofmann's calibre know when they are being patronized and if he suspected he was being baited he would clam up, retreating into his shell for the foreseeable future. McCrary would have to tread lightly. The fact that the agent had done his homework would help him see through Hofmann's lies and might even ingratiate him with the forger who would find it flattering that an FBI profiler had boned up on him.

On arrival at the Utah State Correctional Facility McCrary and his partner Larry were ushered through a steel door into a windowless 10 x 12 ft (3 x 3.7 m) room with bare cement walls. The only items of furniture were the three chairs provided for the interview, one of which the agents set by the door for Hofmann so that he would feel he could leave whenever he pleased. The protocol was that both agents would initially talk to the inmate in turn but when he struck up a rapport with one, the other would withdraw to take notes.

When Hofmann was led in, dressed in a beige prison jumpsuit, he acted as if he suspected a trap. Behind his glasses his eyes

Hofmann took perverse pleasure in deceiving the church elders.

darted nervously between the agents, sizing them up. When McCrary calmly introduced himself Hofmann took a step back. 'My attorneys told me I can't speak to any investigators,' he told them. McCrary assured him they were not investigating his case. They only wanted to talk to him about his experiences in order to understand him better. But Hofmann was no fool. He repeated what he had been prepped to say and backed away again, forcing McCrary to play for time. He reminded Hofmann that they had travelled a long way to see him and that it wouldn't cost him anything to listen. Hofmann gazed coyly at the floor like an embarrassed schoolboy while McCrary patiently and tactfully skirted round the real issue – his crimes, which included the murder of two people with a home-made pipe bomb – and asked him instead about his family and his background, to create the impression that Hofmann was controlling the interview and had the choice whether to respond or not. McCrary casually remarked that he knew Hofmann had financial worries prior to the bombings and must have been under enormous stress at the time. Hofmann raised his eyes and nodded. He'd taken the bait. Psychopaths almost always see themselves as victims of circumstance as it absolves them of any responsibility for their actions. He would have been looking for someone else to blame and now it seemed as if this FBI agent might be a good listener. McCrary repeated the line about how they just wanted to get their facts right in this case and that Hofmann was the only one who could help them do that. That massaged his already over-inflated ego, and when McCrary told Hofmann that he knew he wasn't a naturally callous person and suggested that his motives might have been influenced by his concern for his family, that provided the lifeline the lonely con must have been looking for. After spending 23 hours of every day in his cell since January 1988, he was ready to talk.

The agents 'confessed' that they admired his meticulousness and expertise in crafting the documents. They were careful to mimic their subject's manner and mode of speech like a counsellor who shows empathy even if they do not approve of their client's actions. In this measured way the interview progressed for hour after hour till the time came for lock up and lights out – then it went on into the early hours. The agents learned that Hofmann's entire campaign to discredit the church and enrich himself at their expense had originated with the day he accepted his born-again baptism. He had expected to see the world anew and was bitterly disappointed to discover that nothing had changed. He felt betrayed and hated himself for having been taken in so easily, as he saw it. Anyone else might have swallowed their disappointment and tried another path but he was not a man to be made a fool of. Psychopaths do not accept disappointment gracefully. From that day on he swore the church would reap what it had sown. He would defraud the Mormon organization just as he had been defrauded by utilizing his skills as a master forger and their gullibility. He created authentic documents which contradicted the authorized version of the church's history and sold them to the elders of his local community who dutifully suppressed them to avoid awkward questions and allow the congregation to keep their faith. Hofmann did not see this as fraud or deception. Quite the opposite. He was only deceiving the elders who he believed were fleecing their followers and seducing them into joining their congregation on false pretences. He saw himself as conning the conmen. It was only after his customers began to voice their suspicions that he decided to divert their attention by posting the pipe bombs. The agents noted that when Hofmann described how he made the bombs he began to sweat and exhibit signs of emotional and sexual arousal. The level of detail he recalled was astonishing. It was as if he saw it all again like a movie playing out before his eyes. As he relived the events of the day of the second bombing it was obvious from his words and his manner that the victims were insignificant bit players in his drama. He showed no awareness whatever of the suffering he had caused, or remorse for the second victim who had been the wife of the intended target, an innocent who died because of Hofmann's self-righteous wrath. His psychotic shadow self, suppressed for so long, was now on stage for all to see.

Perpetrator as Profiler

'One side of me says I'd like to talk to her, date her. The other side of me says, I wonder what her head would look like on a stick?'

Ed Kemper

As we have seen, the police are not the only people who use profiling techniques. Criminals do so instinctively whenever they size up a potential victim. Even if they only plan to rob that person, they rarely ambush them without first assessing the risk. How vulnerable is this person? Are they likely to hand over their valuables without a struggle? Sex killers in particular are obsessive individuals who are constantly on the lookout for potential prey to fulfil their fantasy. They never cease to be on the prowl, sizing up locations where they can abduct a victim or carry out an assault with the minimum risk of being observed or interrupted. They'll look at the way the person is dressed and read the non-verbal clues given by their body language. They will rehearse the abduction over and over in their mind and anticipate any problems so they are not fazed by the unexpected. Ed Kemper boasted of how he evaded detection on several occasions by virtue of his practised laid-back demeanour. On one occasion he was pulled over by a police patrolman for having a broken tail light and let off with a warning because he appeared so polite and apologetic. Had the officer insisted on looking in the trunk he would have found two dead bodies and Kemper would not have hesitated to kill him too. Another time Kemper evaded a routine search of his car by joking with a university security guard who let him drive through the gate without a closer look at the two intoxicated companions, one in the passenger seat and one in the rear. In fact neither woman was drunk. They were dying of gunshot wounds.

Kemper's profiling techniques were basic but they were effective. Time after time, lone females would set aside their suspicions and accept a lift from him simply because he would glance at his watch as if considering whether he could spare the time to drop them off. They assumed he was a busy man with a schedule to keep and had nothing else on his mind. The disarmingly charming Ted Bundy practised a variation of this tactic. He would lure his young female victims by wearing a plaster cast on his arm and ask them for assistance which preyed on their natural inclination to help a person in need and lulled them into a false sense of security.

Chapter Four:
Profiling in Practice

'I didn't want to hurt them, I only wanted to kill them.'
David Berkowitz, the 'Son of Sam' killer

Of the nearly 14,000 FBI agents currently employed by the Bureau, only a handful are full-time profilers, all of whom have considerable experience working in violent crime. One of the fortunate handful, Special Agent James T. Clemente, spent ten years in the Bureau honing his skills before being promoted to the BSU based at Quantico. 'It's a think tank mentality,' he told a CBS interviewer in 2005. 'We attack cases from our different perspectives. Profiling is basically reverse engineering in crime. We look at the behaviour that is exhibited at a crime scene and work backwards toward the type of personality who committed that crime ... a typical law-enforcement officer might only see a serial crime once in their career whereas we see them every week.'

Profiling and Patience

Clemente's experience is typical of the profilers who work out of the cramped cinder block offices in the windowless basement, which was originally designed as a bomb-proof emergency headquarters which could be called into service in the event of a national crisis or catastrophe. In addition to his FBI training, he spent a further two years learning the special skills he needed to get inside the heads of serial offenders. At any given day they will have 10 to 15 cases in progress which they euphemistically refer to as research projects.

Special Agent Jim Fitzgerald defines profiling as a combination of art and science with the profiler being required to be a mixture of cop and psychologist. 'We deal with possibilities and probabilities,' he confesses, 'more than with the sure thing. But there is nothing more gratifying in this line of work than knowing that the right person who committed a violent crime has eventually been arrested and convicted and is off the streets.'

Clemente admits that real-life profiling is not as glamorous or exciting as it's depicted on TV where a crime is solved in a single episode. In contrast, profilers can be working on a case for weeks, months or in some cases even years before they are able to solve it. But they are nothing if not persistent. They are prepared to revisit a site on the anniversary of the crime even if it is five years later to see the scene as it was on the day in the hope of picking up the one vital clue they may have missed when the investigation was active. Patient agents have been rewarded on several occasions after they were shrewd enough to stake out the burial site of the victim on the anniversary of their death in the expectation that the killer might visit the grave to gloat or express remorse. One particular murderer who was apprehended in this way at a cemetery in Chicago told the arresting officers, 'I wondered what took you so long.'

On another occasion agents got an unexpected bonus after they put a watch on a dead girl's grave. Instead of catching her killer, they bagged a hit and run driver who came to the cemetery to beg his victim for forgiveness. In the darkness they hadn't noticed that the weeping man was standing next to the grave that they had been watching.

These techniques are now almost routine in cold cases, but only a few years ago the Illinois police still needed convincing that the profiler's hunch would pay off and that the guilt-ridden 'perp' would turn up at the cemetery. They called off a graveside vigil when the stake-out team got tired of sitting in the rain. When they returned the next morning to collect their motion-activated video cameras, they were astonished to discover they had caught a remorseful suspect on film confessing to his crime, but they have no idea who he is.

Profiling Procedure

From a profiler's viewpoint every murder investigation begins with a careful study of the medical examiner's report, which gives the time and cause of death and will describe the nature of the wounds, noting any signs of sexual assault. Next comes a reading of the preliminary police report which describes the crime scene as it looked when the first patrolman arrived. This will be supported by statements from eyewitnesses who might have been present and the crime scene photos which record every angle and significant item at the location. Usually there will also be a diagram showing the position of the body, the location of spent cartridge casings, or a weapon, the position of all doors and windows indicating whether these were open or locked, as well as any other significant details such as blood spatter patterns, the trajectory of bullets and the track of any struggle that might have taken place so that the sequence of events can be recreated. If the crime scene is an exterior location all footprints, tyre tracks and significant geographical features such as footpaths and access roads will be indicated.

An inventory of stolen valuables would be attached together with a list of any notable items that might have no intrinsic value but which might have been taken as souvenirs in case they provide vital clues to the personality of the offender or are pertaining to motive.

If the investigating officer favoured a particular suspect or possessed any other fact they considered pertinent some profilers might ask for them to be written on the back of the photographs or put into a sealed envelope so that they would not be influenced before they had a chance to form their own opinion.

A major serial murder investigation can lose focus by virtue of the sheer volume of information available on each victim, so it is common practice to display the relevant maps and key photos on whiteboards. The maps might be peppered with coloured pins to show the body disposal sites and secondary pick-up or abduction sites. The most important aspect of this visual presentation is ensuring that the victims' photographs and details are displayed in the order in which they were killed and not the order in which the bodies were found. In cases of multiple murder or serial sexual assault it is imperative to see how the offender is evolving and to be able to identify if there is a significant divergence in the pattern of behaviour which could reveal the existence of more than one offender.

Silent Witness

Unless the victim was clearly a target of indiscriminate violence, the team will start by studying their lifestyle, relationships and background in minute detail, because in the absence of a suspect the most significant clue can be their choice of victim. Clemente compares this process to holding a mirror up to the offender because the choice of victim, the manner of the attack, the time the crime took place and the location reveals much about the perpetrator. The choices he makes reflect his personality. The location can tell an investigator where the offender feels comfortable, while the condition of the victim and the crime scene can betray what level of risk he was willing to take.

If a victim has been mutilated an hour or more after the estimated time of death it can indicate that the killer is older and more experienced. It will not be his first murder as he evidently felt sufficiently confident to return to indulge his sadistic fantasy and could be on an escalating cycle of violence.

But it is important for investigators to be able to distinguish between pre- and post-mortem mutilations. It is comparatively simple to determine if a wound has been made post mortem as the incision will be bloodless and the edges of the wound will be dry. Many mutilations of female victims are an attempt at defeminization. Typically a breast might have been cut open or a foreign object inserted in the vagina. But these are not necessarily the acts of a sadistic psychopath. The nature of the offender will be determined by whether or not the mutilations were caused while the victim was alive. If a breast has been cut off or cut open, it would suggest curiosity, as would the insertion of an object in the vagina after death, provided that there is no evidence of force.

The fact that the pathologist needs to establish is whether the offender was probing or humiliating the victim. However, if there is evidence that the breast was cut and the object was inserted while the victim was alive, it would suggest torture. Only the sociopath commits a sadistic assault while the victim is alive. The psychotic will be responsible for the defeminization and the post-mortem acts of curiosity.

The choice of location (open or secluded) and the evidence he leaves behind will suggest whether or not he was forensically aware and of high, low or average intelligence. If the body has been dumped in the open with no attempt to conceal it, the killer is showing contempt for the victim. A body that has been dragged and dumped tells investigators that the perpetrator wanted to delay the discovery until he could be clear of the area and that he felt he had time to cover his tracks. A first-time killer wouldn't be so deliberate. If there were no tracks or prints other than the killer's it would be safe to assume that the body had been carried and placed there. If the corpse was dressed and made presentable with an attempt to restore dignity in death, it could suggest what the Bureau calls 'psychic erasure' or 'restitution'. This remorse or belated attempt to make good would not be evident in psychotics or sociopaths, but in obsessive-compulsive personalities and could well betray the fact that the killer knew the victim personally. The same is true if there is evidence of repeated blows or stab wounds to the face which can betray an attempt to obliterate the victim.

If he had used whatever object was at hand to injure or kill the victim, it would suggest he was a disorganized offender acting on impulse as opposed to an organized offender who would have planned the crime and prepared by bringing burglary tools or a weapon.

Organized vs Disorganized Offenders

Typically the organized offender will possess average or above-average intelligence, be socially and sexually competent, prefer skilled work and will have been the older sibling in a large family. When the background of this offender is examined it invariably reveals that the father had a secure, stable occupation, but the children suffered from inconsistent discipline which gave them mixed messages regarding what is acceptable behaviour. As an adult the organized offender would probably be living with a partner, own a decent, well-maintained reliable car, but be under stress at home or at work. He would probably seek temporary relief in alcohol and this would help him to overcome his inhibitions and give him the nerve to engage his intended victims in conversation, but he would not be so drunk as to be out of control while committing the crime. He would be acutely aware of what he was doing and not fear for the consequences until the full realization of what he had done shocked him back to reality. If so, he might be overcome with remorse and wracked with guilt. He would lose sleep, take time off work, change his appearance and consider leaving town to make a new start once the initial commotion had died down. But he would be haunted by what he had done and would follow the investigation in the news. He may even return to the graveside of his victim to ask forgiveness. He would be particularly vulnerable to suggestion on the anniversary of the crime and on his victim's birthday. Knowing this and his pattern of post-offence behaviour, it is relatively easy to devise strategies to smoke him out (see page 155). But there is a subcategory of organized offender for whom murder is their work. These are the serial killers and rapists who create their own crime kits, including weapons, ligatures, rope, masking tape, binoculars and gloves and even a change of clothes. They tend to be forensically aware and will take extra measures to conceal the body at a separate location. Ed Kemper, John Wayne Gacy, Henry Lee Lucas, Ted Bundy and David Berkowitz were all examples of the organized serial killer, although they all became sloppier as they devolved into disorganized offenders towards the end of their criminal careers.

As FBI agent Roger Depue explained to Bureau biographer Ronald Kessler, 'The organized offender enjoys the predatory aspect of killing – hunting, manipulating and gaining control. He may select a certain kind of weapon and he learns from experience … Because he is so skilled it is difficult to catch him. And when he is caught, everyone says, "I can't believe he did it."'

The Calculating Killer

John List, however, created a category of his own. This 46-year-old, mild-mannered accountant shot his mother, his wife and their three teenage children one morning in December 1971 while a funeral dirge played on an endless loop through the speaker system in the ballroom of their dilapidated New Jersey mansion. Then he calmly organized his orderly disappearance and the creation of a new life and identity in Colorado. He cancelled the milk and his daily newspaper, wrote to the school to tell them the family would be leaving town for a while and turned down the thermostat so that the oil wouldn't run out before the bodies were found (causing the pipes to freeze and burst, creating unnecessary expense for the bank which held the mortgage). When the police broke in several weeks later, they found the children neatly laid out in a row on sleeping bags and their mother's face covered with a cloth. This indicated that the killer was either avoiding the accusing face of the mother or shielding her from the gruesome sight of her dead children. But the identity of the perpetrator in

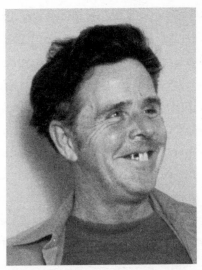

Henry Lee Lucas was an example of the 'organized killer'.

this case was never in doubt. John List had left a full confession, but not for the police – for his Lutheran pastor. He had tried to justify his actions by claiming that he was facing financial ruin and had been driven by the desire to spare his family the indignity of living on welfare by sending them to heaven, but it was clear to investigators that this was a cowardly crime and the real motive was pure self-interest. The uptight, self-righteous List could not bear the shame of losing face in front of his family so he disposed of them and set off to start a new one elsewhere. Had he acted in a moment of madness he would have probably committed suicide after he realized what he had done, or turned himself in and expressed revulsion over his actions, but the autopsy revealed that the time of death was different for each victim, ruling out the initial assumption that it had been a mass murder. List had shot his wife and mother in the morning then, later in the day, had picked up his daughter, driven her home then shot her in cold blood in the back of the head. He repeated the routine with his youngest son, but was surprised when John Jnr returned home early. His murder was messier. He had been shot ten times with bullets from two guns. This was not the act of a deranged maniac. List was deliberate, calculating and in control and therefore he was judged to be legally sane. After having evaded justice and the consequences of his actions for a staggering 20 years, he was found guilty on five counts of first degree murder and sentenced to five consecutive terms of life imprisonment.

In contrast, the typical disorganized offender would be of below-average intelligence, socially and sexually inadequate, be employed in an unskilled job, if at all, and be unable to sustain a serious relationship. He would therefore be likely to be living alone or with an elder brother, sister or his elderly parents, probably near the crime scene as his offences would have been spontaneous and opportunistic. As a child, he will have been the youngest in a financially and emotionally insecure family whose parents subjected him to harsh discipline and abuse. He would not need alcohol or drugs to tip him over the edge as he would be an emotionally unstable and volatile personality whose outbursts of violence could be triggered by the smallest perceived insult, but he may over-indulge in drink and drugs after the offence if only because he has no other pleasure in life. He would be in an emotional turmoil during the crime and therefore unpredictable and incapable of staging a scene effectively or eradicating evidence, although he may make a clumsy, ineffectual attempt to do both. This in itself would reveal the type of offender investigators should be seeking. His weapon would be a weapon of opportunity

John List was a mild-mannered accountant.

which he would leave at the crime scene with the body and which he would make no effort to conceal.

Lacking a conscience and being legally insane, he would show no interest in following the case unless it was to collect press cuttings to boost his lack of self-esteem. Obviously the more mentally disturbed he is, the more disorganized will be the scene he leaves behind. He is also likely to linger at the crime scene to mutilate or have sex with the corpse.

Richard Trenton Chase is often cited as a prime example of the disorganized offender. He was a paranoid schizophrenic who butchered his randomly chosen victims and drank their blood in the belief that his own was turning to sand. Ironically, the jury were afraid to find him insane because they knew that if they did he would be institutionalized and could be released at some future date. Instead they found him guilty and the judge sentenced him to die in the gas chamber. But before the state could rid themselves of him he took an overdose of sleeping pills and died the same day.

Although much of a profiler's day is spent poring over photographs and sifting through reports to familiarize themselves with the facts, it is considered vital that they go to the scene as soon as possible after being assigned to the case. Agents need to view the scene and the setting for themselves. An offender will choose a secluded site for a reason and it may not always be the obvious one – that he does not want to be seen committing the crime or he needs to hide the body. In 1979 the Trailside Killer was finally identified and convicted of murdering several female hikers in San Francisco's national parks after profiler John Douglas told the local police to look for a suspect with a speech impediment. His pronouncement was greeted with a mixture of astonishment and cynicism, but his reasoning was sound. The murders had taken place at secluded mountain locations rather than in the city which suggested that the UNSUB (unknown subject) was acutely self-conscious and believed he could not persuade young women to go with him voluntarily. The fact that he had to rely on a surprise attack from behind even in an isolated location indicated that he must have felt ashamed to engage a stranger face to face. The first two victims had been found on their knees, one with a bullet in the head, the other stabbed to death, indicative of a ritual killing – they had been begging for their lives when he killed them, which would be consistent with a killer who needed to dominate and control to compensate for his handicap. Of course, this disability could be something other than a stammer, but it was highly unlikely that he would be afflicted with a serious physical disability otherwise he would not have been able to subdue the hikers who were all physically fit. Facial disfigurement could also be ruled out as none of the witnesses had reported seeing anyone in the area at the time to whom that would apply. When a suspect was finally arrested, after having been identified by a man he had shot and left for dead, he was found to have a severe stutter.

In a very different case a little girl had been murdered in a densely populated suburb and the local police were at a loss as to where to start scouring for suspects. The FBI was called in and began by taking aerial photographs. From these they were able to deduce that it was extremely unlikely that an outsider had come upon the girl's house by chance as it was located in the centre of a maze of cul de sacs and side streets. It was far more likely that a neighbour had been watching her for some time until his obsession overwhelmed him and he lost control of himself.

When Is a Crime Not a Crime?

The more experienced profilers will admit to having developed what almost amounts to a sixth sense so that they can tell when a scene has been staged or a crime has been created to cover for something else. In his autobiography, *Mindhunter*, John Douglas gives several examples of cases that aroused his suspicions. The first was where a number of spousal murders were staged to look like cases of lethal product tampering, but when they were investigated they didn't conform to the classic pattern. If the number of incidents of alleged tampering were comparatively few and localized it would suggest the products might have been contaminated to camouflage the intended target. This suspicion would be strengthened if it was subsequently discovered that there had been problems between one of the victims and their partner or another family member with access to the product.

Forensics will also be able to determine whether the poison or contaminant used in a suspicious death is part of the same batch as that used by the extortionist. If not, it could be that the extortionist is not responsible for the suspicious death. Even extortionists leave their personal signature on the product they have contaminated which a copy-cat killer will not be able to replicate.

Kidnappings are another challenge for the profiler, who must tread softly when determining whether an alleged victim is really the injured party or has faked their own abduction or that of their child.

In one memorable case in Oregon a young female student had apparently been abducted after having been stalked for several weeks. She had also reported receiving threatening phone calls. Douglas' suspicions were aroused by the fact that no one else had seen the stalker although the 'victim's' family had searched the area immediately after she reported each incident, and no one else had been at home when the threatening calls had been received. Moreover, when the police tapped the line, the calls stopped. Just before the alleged abduction the woman reported having been

John Douglas sifts through some photo files.

assaulted by a mysterious man in the car park of a restaurant and warned at gunpoint not to inform the police. Surely, if he had cornered his intended victim alone in a public place without any witnesses he would not have allowed her to leave but would have abducted her there and then. But the clincher came when it was discovered that the victim had been having problems with her father concerning financial support for her newly born baby, her grades had suffered and she was scheduled to take her final exams the week she was kidnapped.

In cases like this it is important that the police do not share their suspicions with the family, who will be under extreme emotional stress. It could be a genuine case of abduction and the victim's body could be discovered at any time. Anything that might add to the family's torment is to be avoided. In this particular case, Agent Douglas advised the father to make a public appeal through the media in which he would stress his love for his daughter and appeal to her abductor to free her. If Douglas' suspicions were right she would turn up a couple of days later, suffering minor injuries and with a story straight out of a cheap crime novel. The end of this episode played out precisely as Douglas had predicted. But instead of being accused of having wasted police time and putting her family through hell, the police made it clear they understood that she was having problems and was under pressure. They assured her she would not be prosecuted but would instead be offered counselling. When the girl heard this she broke down and confessed to having faked her own abduction.

A person's choice of language can be another clue in determining when they are covering up their involvement in a crime. If, for example, a parent switches from referring to their children as my kids or our kids to the kids it is likely that he or she is unconsciously distancing themselves from their part in the children's murder, abduction or abuse.

In another case Agent Gregg McCrary investigated the alleged abduction of a toddler whose mother claimed she had been forced to leave him in the lobby of her apartment building while she went to the rest room. When she returned he was nowhere to be seen. The only clue was one of his mittens discarded in the car park. The police wasted no time in activating their child abduction procedure which included bringing in dozens of officers to conduct a thorough search of the area, but afterwards failing to find him they took the precaution of giving the mother a polygraph test, which she passed. The next day the mother received the missing mitten in the mail. Everything seemed to confirm her story, but McCrary smelt a rat. The package containing the mitten did not come with a ransom demand and there was something fishy about the 911 emergency call which the mother had made on the day of the abduction. She had told the operator that her son had been kidnapped, a word that a frantic parent would be unlikely to use at such a moment. They would be in denial, hoping that the child had simply wandered off, in which case they would say that he was missing or lost. By using the word kidnapped the mother expects a specific scenario to be played out, yet has no reason to assume the worst.

McCrary was convinced that the child was dead and that the mother had killed him. The police were sceptical. How could he be so sure? There were several paedophiles active in the area, any one of whom could have taken the child. This is when the behavioural psychology kicks in. McCrary explained that no mother would leave her young child unattended in a public area while she went to the bathroom. She would take him with her or arrange for someone she knew in the building to keep an eye on the child. But the crucial clue came with the mitten. A kidnapper wouldn't send an item as proof that he had abducted someone without adding a ransom note or a threat of some kind, while a paedophile or someone who stole the child to bring it up as their own wouldn't need to prove that they had taken the child. The mother already knows it has been taken. Like the girl from Oregon who had faked her own abduction, the mother in this case had staged the kidnapping according to what she thought a real kidnapping would be and it was obviously a sham. But she had been able to pass the lie detector test because she could justify what she had done in her own mind. She was a young unmarried mother who had become involved with a man who didn't want another man's child. So she killed her own son and faked the abduction to divert suspicion from herself. A second polygraph test treated her as a suspect and asked more direct questions which produced a completely different set of results.

The significance of this case is that McCrary would have created an identical profile had the police discovered the child's body at the outset and not been distracted by the hoax abduction.

Staging a Crime Scene

When the mother eventually led the police to the body it had been buried in the woods in its snowsuit, wrapped in a blanket and covered with a thick plastic bag as if it was being insulated from the cold. It revealed that despite her disturbed state of mind the mother was still concerned for the welfare of the child and was acting out of remorse and guilt. A stranger would not have gone to such lengths to make the infant 'comfortable'.

A similar example of staging occurred in Cartersville, Georgia on Boxing Day, 1980. The body of Linda Dover was found wrapped in a blanket in the crawl space under the house she had once shared with her ex-husband Larry. She had suffered blunt force trauma to her head and face and multiple stab wounds. It was clear to John Douglas that this was another staged scene. There was no evidence of sexual assault and yet an effort had been made to make it look as if she had been assaulted. Her jeans and panties had been pulled down and her shirt and bra pushed up, exposing her breasts. The blanket served no purpose other than to preserve her modesty which indicated that the killer was ashamed at the thought that strangers might see her in such a state. Moreover, there was no reason for a stranger to have dragged the body from the upstairs bedroom, where blood stains indicated she had been killed, to the crawl space under the property. The only explanation could be that it had been hidden there to save her young son from seeing his mother's corpse. Less than a year later Larry Dover was convicted and sentenced to life imprisonment for her murder.

John Douglas has compared the process of reading a crime scene to an actor's initial reading of a script in which they look beyond the words for the subtext to understand what the scene is really about. A good example of this technique occurred on 30 August 1986 in Pennsylvania when police were called to a reported break-in at the home of a successful young dentist just after seven that morning. They found 33-year-old Dr Edward Wolsieffer downstairs in a semi-conscious state claiming that he had been partially strangled then knocked unconscious by an intruder who he had followed downstairs. His brother Neil, who lived across the road, was by his side having been called the moment Edward had recovered consciousness. Edward told the officers he feared for the safety of his wife, Betty, and their 5-year-old daughter who had been asleep in their upstairs bedrooms when the alleged attack occurred. But each time he had attempted to mount the stairs he felt weak and his brother had had to stay with him. The officers searched the house but found no sign of an intruder. When they entered the master bedroom, they found Betty lying lifeless on the floor next to the bed with her nightgown pushed up to her waist. From the bluish tinge to her face, the foam around her mouth and the bruises on her neck it was evident she had been strangled. The child was found unharmed in her bed and when woken told the police she had heard nothing that morning and had slept soundly. That in itself was suspicious, but then there were a number of physical anomalies which contradicted Wolsieffer's version of events. Outside at the rear of the house, a ladder had been placed under the open window of the second-floor bedroom, but the rungs were the wrong way round and the ladder itself looked too flimsy to take the weight of a grown man. Besides, there were no indentations in the soft soil or on the guttering where it rested and no dew, mud or grass on the rungs, which one would expect to find if someone had used the ladder in the early hours of the morning. Nothing of value had been taken during the alleged burglary and, although Dr Wolsieffer had suffered a blow to the back of his head, there were no marks on his neck to support his claim that he had been strangled. Neil could have inflicted the superficial blow or the dentist could have deliberately banged his head on the corner of a bookcase or cupboard. The deeper the police probed into Edward Wolsieffer's story the more incredible it sounded: and then his late wife's friends provided what appeared to be the motive. Shortly before her death, Betty had told them that she was going to give Edward an ultimatum: to stop his womanizing or she would seek a separation.

However, as in many cases of this type, circumstantial evidence and hearsay is rarely sufficient to justify charging a suspect let alone secure a conviction. Another way would have to be found to force Dr Wolsieffer to confess. Attention turned to his brother, Neil, whose testimony would be crucial in supporting Edward's alibi, but Neil refused to submit to a polygraph test and his story changed as often as his brother's. Eventually, under pressure from the media and Betty's family, he agreed to cooperate, but was killed in a road accident on the morning he was due to be formally interviewed by the police. He had overshot an intersection on a road leading out of town, which suggested that it may have been suicide or he may have been trying to get away. Whatever the reason, even his death failed to persuade Edward to confess.

When John Douglas read through the voluminous police reports at Quantico 18 months after the murder, he knew he was looking at another typical staged crime scene and he was confident that he could prove it.

The police had named Dr Wolsieffer as the prime suspect so a standard offender profile was not required. Instead Douglas analyzed the behaviour of the fictitious intruder and discovered that his actions were entirely illogical if his intent had been burglary or murder. The burglary scenario was implausible in the extreme. No professional thief would break into a house in broad daylight at a weekend when the owners were almost certain to be at home. The presence of the two cars in the driveway would have been sufficient to frighten off even the most audacious thief. If the motive had been murder, why did the intruder not bring a weapon? Instead he strangled the wife with his hands and apparently garrotted the husband before hitting him over the head with whatever came to hand. Strangulation is a very personal method of murder rarely favoured by strangers. And why was the wife killed but the husband allowed to live despite the chance that he might be able to identify his assailant? If the intention had been either burglary or murder, it was inconceivable that the murder scene would have been staged like a rape, especially when there was no physical evidence of sexual assault.

Furthermore, what kind of thief enters through a second-storey window and then proceeds to go downstairs without checking out the upstairs bedrooms? And after he had supposedly surprised and rendered the husband unconscious, why would he leave the gun when there was a chance the man of the house might regain consciousness and use it against him?

Edward and Neil's behaviour was also inconsistent with their story. Even if Edward was too weak to climb the stairs, surely he would have insisted that his brother should see if his wife and daughter were safe. The fact that he didn't suggests that he knew what they would find upstairs.

Posing

In both of the quoted examples the body had been posed to give the false impression that the victim had been sexually assaulted. But for many killers, arranging their lifeless victim like a mannequin can be their sole reason for committing the crime. Many serial killers and sex offenders are inadequate individuals who feel driven to avenge themselves on those they imagine have spurned or humiliated them. In turn, they will pose their victims in a way that degrades and dehumanizes them. It is their one chance to exercise some form of control over others. It becomes the distinguishing feature of their crimes and what is known as their signature.

The significance of posing as part of a killer's signature can be seen in a landmark case of 1991. George Russell Jnr was a handsome, well-educated, urbane black man in his 30s with many friends and female admirers. When he was arrested for killing three white women, the Seattle police could not believe they had the right man. But Russell was also a professional thief with a lengthy criminal record. Inter-racial sex crimes were still extremely rare and it was thought that a jury would be predisposed to acquit Russell on this factor alone. That was why a confident public defender petitioned the judge to have the cases tried separately as there was insufficient evidence to secure a conviction in the first murder and no evidence to tie the three killings together. The prosecution had to prove a connection between all three crimes or risk an acquittal. At this point FBI profiler Steve Etter was approached and asked to explain how the murders were connected. He pointed out that the method was the same in all three incidents, which had taken place within a seven-week period, and that an offender would be unlikely to alter his MO within such a small time-frame unless something had gone drastically wrong during one of the attacks. But the distinguishing feature was the posing of the bodies which was not necessary, but gratuitous. It expresses the killer's anger and need to exercise power but it is also intended to send a contemptuous message to the authorities. In the Russell case the naked corpses had been arranged with the aim of degrading the victim. And this signature had become progressively more pronounced. The first victim had been left by a dumpster with her legs crossed and hands clasped. The second was arranged on a bed with red high heels on her feet, her legs spread and a pillow over her head. A rifle barrel had been inserted into her vagina. The third victim was spread-eagled on her bed with a sex toy in her mouth and a sex manual under her arm. Outwardly these women appeared to have been murdered by three different individuals, but if each was seen as conforming to a pattern of escalating behaviour it is clear they were all killed and posed by the same man. During the pre-trial hearing, the chief criminal investigator Bob Keppel testified that posing itself is extremely rare. Of more than a thousand murder cases which he had been personally involved in, only about ten had featured posing and none had the elements replicated in all three of the killings Russell had been accused of committing.

After four days of deliberation the jury found Russell guilty on one count of first degree murder and two counts of aggravated first degree murder. The judge sentenced him to life imprisonment without parole.

The Significance of the Signature

'It should be noted the above analysis is not a substitute for a thorough and well-planned investigation and should not be *considered all-inclusive. The information provided is based upon reviewing, analyzing and researching criminal cases similar to the case submitted by the requesting agency. The final analysis is based upon the probabilities, noting, however, that no two criminal acts or criminal personalities are exactly alike and therefore the offender at times may not always fit the profile in every category.'*

Standard FBI disclaimer

As the standard FBI disclaimer acknowledges, there is no template to cover all categories of offender. Criminals are individuals too and no two serial killers or extortionists are alike. There must be something distinctive for the investigator to identify as the offender's signature.

It is important to make a distinction between an offender's signature and their modus operandi. Their MO is simply their method of operating, the procedure they follow in pursuit of their crime. It can cover their choice of target, their preferred location, the tools they selected, the means by which they subdued their victim or their method of gaining entry to a property. A burglar's MO may, for example, involve using flypaper to collect glass fragments when he breaks a window pane to prevent them from falling to the ground and alerting the occupier. If the police find fragments of flypaper at several break-ins they can narrow down their shortlist of suspects to those who are known to use flypaper. However, an offender can change their MO for any number of reasons, one of the most common being that improved security has made the old preferred method impractical, or they may graduate to another type of offence, such as when a burglar graduates to rape or murder. Identifying the motive can determine whether an offender subsequently stands trial for manslaughter or for murder as it reveals what their intention was at the time of the crime.

A signature, on the other hand, is the offender's trademark, his calling card, something that he feels compelled to do to fulfil a need regardless of the nature of the crime. It may even put him at greater risk of getting caught, but like an addict he must do it in order to relieve the tension which drives him to commit the offence in the first place. It may involve ritual display of the corpse, torture, mutilation, foreign object insertion, cannibalism, necrophilia, or what is known as overkill, that is inflicting injuries way beyond those necessary to cause death. In these cases sex has become equated with violence and vice versa, leaving murder the only form of release this individual can conceive of.

Whatever the signature may be it will not directly further the commission of the crime. While an offender's choice of murder weapon, victim and location may change over the years, their signature will remain constant, although it can develop. Mutilations, for example, may become more extreme. The crimes of the reformed Austrian murderer Jack Unterweger, for example, were years and continents apart, but he was eventually condemned for a second series of slayings when it was demonstrated that he had used a distinctive knot in the ligatures with which he had strangled all his victims. After Unterweger had been sentenced to life in prison, profiler Gregg McCrary warned that Jack was likely to take his own life as this controlling personality type always has to have the last word. But the guards did not watch him as closely as they might and Unterweger garrotted himself in his cell with a cord from his jumpsuit using the same ligature with which he had strangled his victims. Someone dryly observed that it was his best murder.

Unfortunately, there are still many law enforcement officers who will assume that if there is a variation in MO between one crime and another very similar crime in the same area they will have been committed by two different offenders. This was the fatal mistake made by the police investigating a series of prostitute murders in Rochester, New York in 1989. Detectives failed to identify the signature common to all the murders and instead divided the crimes according to the type of victim, which included both black and white women, some of whom were prostitutes while others were not. Instead of combining their energy and resources in the pursuit of one offender, they charged off in three different directions.

Jack Unterweger enjoyed his moment in the spotlight.

But it is not only serial killers who often feel compelled to personalize the crime scene. Any offender who commits a crime in order to compensate for their inadequacies, or assert their supposed superiority, will use the opportunity to make a statement which will be as distinctive as their fingerprint.

A prime example of the difference between MO and signature is highlighted by two apparently similar cases of bank robbery in which the robbers forced the bank staff and their customers to strip naked. When caught, a robber in Texas explained that he had ordered the people to undress so that they would be so preoccupied with their own predicament that they would be less likely to remember his face. That was his MO. In a separate incident in Michigan, a bank robber forced his hostages to strip, pair off and simulate sex while he photographed them. This had no bearing on the robbery but was done for the robber's perverse pleasure. That was his signature. It was an irrational compulsion, and was peculiar to him. As profilers have often said when questioned on the witness stand, no two crimes are exactly alike, but when an offender has an identifiable signature there will always be similarities linking their crimes while at the same time distinguishing them from the thousands of other crimes in the same category.

There Is Nothing Like Experience

There is much more to profiling than understanding the basics of criminal psychology. Even the most well-meaning psychologists can unintentionally mislead an investigation if they do not have sufficient law enforcement experience to put the clues into context.

FBI profiler Larry Ankrom was once asked for his opinion on an alleged rape case which had run out of steam. A year earlier a university psychology professor had been invited to compile a profile on an UNSUB following a woman's claim that she had been raped by a stranger. The professor's lengthy analysis, based solely on textbook examples, detailed the unknown offender's educational background, criminal history and personal habits and had kept the police busy following false trails for a year. Agent Ankrom and his colleague Gregg McCrary studied the files independently and both came to the same conclusion – the rape allegation was a hoax. The fictitious offender was a two-dimensional character who could only exist in a badly written novel. When they presented their conclusions to the police they admitted that they had suspected the allegation was false for some time but the professor's profile had been so detailed that they had felt obliged to act upon it. When they confronted the woman with their suspicions, using a tactful, non-confrontational strategy specially developed for interviewing pseudo victims, she admitted she had made the whole story up.

Even when a crime has been committed, inexperienced and wannabe profilers can do more harm than good. One of John Douglas' early cases involved the murder of an elderly woman in her home in Oregon. She had been stabbed with a pencil which led the local clinical psychologist to surmise that she had been attacked by an ex-con as prisoners frequently use sharpened pencils as weapons, as there is little else to hand. Douglas was of a different opinion. Experience had taught him that the older the victim, the younger will be the offender, as juveniles seek out the most vulnerable victims. He convinced the police that they should be looking for an inexperienced juvenile offender as it was a daylight crime, nothing of value had been stolen and the injuries to the vulnerable, elderly victim exhibited all the signs of overkill. An ex-con would have been in command of the situation whereas a youth might panic when challenged and react disproportionately to the threat by grabbing whatever came to hand and lashing out. Some time later the police charged a 16-year-old boy who had been canvassing the neighbourhood for charity contributions which he was not authorized to collect.

More recently a certain section of the academic and scientific community have been advocating the introduction of specialized computer programs to collate data with a view to pinpointing an offender's point of origin. But although geographical analysis of abduction sites, dump sites and secondary crime scenes can be instructive, profilers are wary of relying on statistics to solve crimes.

'Profiling is like writing,' says Douglas. 'You can give a computer all the rules of grammar and syntax and style, but it still can't write the book ... The fact of the matter is profiling and crime scene analysis is a lot more than simply inputting data and crunching it through. To be a good profiler, you have to be able to evaluate a wide range of evidence and data. But you also have to be able to walk in the shoes of both the offender and the victim.'

Mind Games

There is more to profiling than providing the police with a sketch of the perpetrator's personality. Besides, even the most accurate profile can have its limitations, particularly when there are a number of suspects who would fit the bill. In such cases – when the trail of clues has run cold – profiling has been used to devise strategies to draw the offender out into the open. It is what law enforcement calls going 'proactive'.

Luring the Prey Into the Open

Profilers might advise local law enforcement agencies to organize a series of public meetings to evaluate the danger to public safety and publicize what they know about the offender in the belief that he will attend, being unable to resist the temptation to assess the level of threat he has created. Detectives would then have a chance to interview any individuals who matched the age and physical characteristics of the profile and take names and addresses for further investigation.

Another productive strategy might be to announce that a witness has come forward in the belief that this could flush out the offender who could be keen to explain why he had been seen in the area at the time in the hope of eliminating himself from the inquiry.

But there is no guidebook to tell investigators how to flush out an UNSUB. They have to act on their own initiative, creating strategies based on their personal assessment of the situation. In one case where a killer was thought to be among a large number of manual workers in an isolated region of Canada, all of whom frequented the local bar, the owner had the brilliant idea of raffling a TV set in the hope of securing his customers' names and addresses. In the notorious Atlanta Child Murders investigation FBI profilers advised local law enforcement to organize a fund-raising concert for the victims and advertise for volunteer security guards with suitable experience in the belief that the UNSUB would apply so that he could enjoy his notoriety. He was thought to be a police buff who would seize any opportunity to be in on the investigation. In neither the Atlanta nor the Canadian case were the proactive strategies acted upon, but in the latter the profile proved right on the money. The perpetrator, Wayne Williams, had once been arrested for impersonating a police officer and even drove a refurbished police vehicle fitted with scanners, so that he could eavesdrop on police radio traffic and get to the crime scenes to take photographs.

Flushing Out an Extortionist

Product tampering presents the profiler with a unique problem in that the victims are chosen at random, there is no crime scene in the accepted sense and the motive is often unclear. Unless the extortionist expresses a grievance in their communications, investigators can only guess at who the intended target might be – the manufacturer, a specific retailer, or society in general. In such cases conventional profiling is of little use, but proactive profiling and a touch of psychological pressure can flush out the perpetrator before his campaign can claim an innocent life.

Profilers will act on the assumption that the individual responsible for such cowardly, impersonal acts is not interested in knowing who drew the short straw. If they can be made aware of the impact they have had on one individual and their family it may persuade them to call off their campaign or maybe even surrender themselves to the police. Extortionists are only concerned with expressing their anger and creating a climate of fear which fuels their bruised egos and gives them the illusion of power. So the first step would be to have the local newspapers publish photographs of the victims with a story detailing the suffering that their families had been put through in the hope that it might prick the perpetrator's conscience.

The second phase might be to lure the perpetrator to one specific store by having the manager boast on TV how he has improved security and now defies any extortionist to tamper with the stock on his shelves. It has been proven that some extortionists simply can't resist a challenge like this and will walk straight into the trap. A variation on this tactic might see the authorities respond to a tip-off at a particular store which turns out to have been a false alarm. Then, in the glare of the TV cameras, the chief investigator would claim that his swift action had frightened off the extortionist which would be taken as a challenge, luring him into the trap.

And all the while the police would be advised to issue positive statements to keep the pressure on the extortionist and break down his resistance and ability to cope.

Interrogation Techniques

As every law enforcement professional knows there is more chance of securing a conviction if you have a confession. Forensic evidence can be compromised and eyewitnesses can retract their testimony or have their credibility questioned in court by a smart lawyer, but as crucial as it can be to have a signed confession, it is imperative that a suspect is not interrogated too soon. It is not enough to be familiar with the facts of the case. An interviewer also needs to know the history and psychological make-up of the suspect. Have they readily confessed to other crimes they have been accused of, or are they impervious to pressure? Have they ever made a false confession in the past and, if so, what reason was given? Some impressionable or disturbed individuals are prone to confess to crimes they have not committed merely to appease their accuser or bring themselves the attention they desperately crave. If they have a criminal record, what does it reveal about their motives? Unless the interviewer knows why the suspect committed his crimes they are groping in the dark. It is like trying to make sense of a set of statistics without knowing the context or their possible application. It may pay to release the suspect after the first interview, keeping him on the hook like a fish until you are ready to reel him in and present him with the facts which will make a denial more difficult. The reasoning behind this tactic is that at the initial interview he will be on the defensive and both sides will spend much of the time sizing each other up. At a second interview he will be more relaxed, a rapport will have been established and he will be assuming that this session will consist of more routine questioning and he will be expecting to be released for a second time. He may become arrogant and careless, letting slip some crucial clue that will catch him in a lie.

The second interview should ideally be staged at night as this is the time when he is likely to be tired and vulnerable. The timing also signals that the police are serious and may even have unearthed a vital witness or clue that merits their prime suspect being dragged out of bed in the middle of the night. The killer's conscience and his fears will be working overtime. There's no scheduled lunch break or obvious cut-off point and the night can seem very, very long to a guilty man. If he's scared of being photographed or paraded in front of the press – this applies particularly to child molesters and those who might be expected to feel an element of shame – they will be under added pressure to confess before the morning.

If more than one force was involved in the investigation it could be productive to have officers from all of these present to demonstrate that he is facing a combined force who will not rest until this matter is resolved.

The scene can also be set as dramatically as on a stage, with low lighting and stacks of files on the table he will be sitting at, all labelled with his name. Even if these are empty, it will give the impression that there is an overwhelming amount of hard evidence against him. And for the final melodramatic touch the weapon found at the scene or any other significant object in the case should be placed to the side so that he will have to turn his head to look at it. If he does so, it signals that he recognizes it and is aware that the detectives are also aware of its significance although they will not have pointed it out or made any reference to it.

If it's a murder case or involves a serious assault, sexual or otherwise, it can be worth suggesting that the victim may have been partly to blame for the situation getting out of hand. This may sound repulsive, but it may be necessary to give the suspect an opening as few will be willing to admit their responsibility from the outset. It often has to be teased out of them, bit by bit, as the layers of lies they have built around the event to protect themselves are peeled away.

Penetrating the Labyrinth –
Coaxing a Killer into Making a Confession

When 19-year-old meat factory worker Paul Kenneth Bostock walked into Blackbird Road Police Station in Leicester, England, on 3 May 1985 in order to eliminate himself from a double murder enquiry detectives were faced with a difficult dilemma. How could they coax a confession from a suspect who was thought to have blocked out the memories of the crimes he had in all probability committed?

The teenager neatly fitted both the physical description given to detectives of a stranger seen on a footpath near where the second body was found as well as the psychological profile provided by Dr Paul Britton, England's foremost criminal psychologist. Bostock was of above average height – 6 ft 5 in (1.96 m) tall and powerfully built, weighing in at a formidable 15 stone (95 kg). He lived with his parents, worked with knives, was a fitness fanatic and, as the police later discovered, he surrounded himself with weapons and violent sadomasochistic images in the form of posters, graphic comics and self-made drawings, many depicting women being tortured. But he appeared to be genuinely unaware of his dreadful crimes although he became visibly uncomfortable when asked to account for his movements on the previous Saturday, the night of the most recent murder, and he contradicted himself on several significant points.

This was not the first time Bostock had been interviewed by detectives during their investigation into the murders of 33-year-old Caroline Osborne and 21-year-old Amanda Weedon. He had been grilled no less than three times and allowed to leave after each session having supplied a satisfactory alibi.

Bostock appeared to know nothing of the killings, but he may have been shamming to avoid facing the enormity of what he had done. If his blackout was genuine it would have been because he had been effectively sleepwalking when his violent shadow-self had committed the crimes, then retreated into his unconscious leaving the teenager as bemused as everyone else in the city. To extract a confession Dr Britton would have to penetrate the dark recesses of Bostock's mind and confront the killer who had taken refuge there.

But he would have to tread carefully. If Britton forced Bostock to face his own demons too soon the shock might force the two facets of the teenager's personality to split permanently with the guilty half retreating further into the uncharted regions of the mind from which it could never be retrieved. The other innocent half would never accept what he had done and Bostock would be confined in a mental institution for the remainder of his life. Without a confession justice would be thwarted, the victims' families would be denied closure and Bostock himself would lose any hope he might have of recovery.

Circling the Suspect

The technique Britton chose to use in his examination of the suspected double murderer is known as 'penetrating the labyrinth'. It involves approaching the subject in ever-decreasing circles in the same way that an analyst might tease out a new patient's medical history. The interrogator needs to establish a rapport and gain the suspect's trust so that when the latter is ready to confess it will be as if he is confiding in someone he believes can help him. He needs to know that the interrogator wants to understand him and the reason why he did what he is accused of. He knows there will be a consequence, that he has been found out, but he needs to be secure in the belief that the interviewer will not turn on him and show revulsion when he is ready to admit what he has done. The fact that Bostock had been interviewed previously and managed to convince detectives of his innocence means that he had created a story which was difficult for him to retract. He would lose face if he was challenged on the facts and forced to admit that he had lied. Instead he would have to be encouraged to reconsider his version of events and, most important of all, be assured that he would not be condemned for his alleged deviant sexual behaviour. He would only crack if he believed he had the ear of someone who had considerable experience with compulsive disorders and was not easily shocked.

When the detectives entered the interview room at Blackbird Road they found the suspect in co-operative mood. He was neither arrogant nor aggressive, but defensive as if he was frightened of being forced to face what lay just beneath the surface of his mind, like the memory of a bad dream. Bostock repeatedly asked

Paul Britton, author of The Jigsaw Man *and Britain's top criminal psychologist.*

if his parents had been informed that he was being questioned yet again and what, if anything, they were being told about the case. His concern for them indicated that he was wrestling with guilt which he couldn't afford to acknowledge for fear of bringing shame on his family. Britton had considered the possibility that Bostock had created a fantasy for himself in which he was merely a detached observer of these crimes and that he had lived the lie for so long that he now believed it. His advice to the detectives was therefore to be non-confrontational. They would have to assume that Bostock was willing to assist the police but needed help in recalling what was difficult for him to acknowledge.

So the interview began with detectives asking Bostock innocuous but detailed questions about his childhood, his schooldays and his friends. In this way suspects get used to recalling events in fine detail so that when they are finally led to discussing the crime they don't have to change gear from speaking in generalities to recalling specific facts as the discontinuity could break their train of thought.

When Bostock felt uncomfortable as he came closer to discussing the murders he would claim that he couldn't remember or wasn't at the location, which told them that he wasn't ready to unburden himself. So, on Dr Britton's advice, they backtracked before returning to the subject in the expectation that each time the suspect would reveal more detail until he had admitted too much to go back. When Bostock contradicted his earlier version of events he was not accused of lying, but the new version was simply acknowledged and he was asked to elaborate upon it. When he admitted to being on the path at the crucial time and seeing the victim, having previously denied being in the vicinity, he was encouraged to elaborate. What was she wearing? Where exactly was she standing?

When the confession eventually came it was with evident relief. Bostock was allowed to tell his side of the story without being interrupted or contradicted. This too was part of the strategy. Only after he had unburdened himself was he questioned on specific points or picked up on apparent contradictions.

But the detectives were curious. Why had he chosen the second girl, Amanda Weedon, rather than others who were at the same location that day? Bostock thought for a second then replied, 'Because she had red shoes.'

At his trial in June 1986 Bostock pleaded guilty to both murders and was sentenced to life imprisonment.

Author's note: Dr Paul Britton's credibility came in for serious media criticism after a speculative profile he compiled was used as a basis for the prosecution of Colin Stagg in the Rachel Nickell murder case in the 1990s. Rachel had been fatally assaulted on Wimbledon Common, south London in July 1992. When the case came to court it was thrown out by the judge on the grounds that the police had used excessive zeal to entrap Stagg despite having no forensic evidence to link him to the crime. Their main reason for arresting Stagg was their assertion that he fitted the profile provided by Dr Britton, but the judge determined that the profile was essentially intuitive and not based on physical evidence. Former FBI profiler Robert Ressler, who assisted the British police in the investigation, later spoke in defence of Dr Britton. 'The public's perception of that case is wrong. The perception was that the profile was improper or that it caused the case to be thrown out. What was wrong was that the court criticized the technique of entrapment.' Despite this, Dr Britton remains a significant figure in the history of criminal profiling in the UK and his experiences using techniques such as that described above continue to be of value to criminologists around the world.

Trial and Error – Unmasking the Monster

There is nothing in the FBI rulebook that states agents cannot play mind games too. Once J. Edgar Hoover was gone, the kid gloves were off and agents felt free to use any legal means at their disposal to get the job done.

On one memorable occasion a racist killer was on trial for murder in Alaska and was presenting himself each day to the court as a model citizen who had been wrongly accused. The FBI agents assigned to the case were seriously worried that his performance was winning over the jury so they persuaded a black colleague to sit next to the defendant's girlfriend and appear very friendly towards her. It didn't take long for the man to lose his composure in the witness box and show his true colours.

The case against Wayne Williams, accused of the Atlanta Child Murders in 1982, was an altogether tougher nut to crack. In court the former disc jockey presented himself as a mild-mannered, softly spoken amiable witness and his attorney Al Binder capitalized on his client's unimposing demeanour. At a crucial point in the trial Binder turned to the jury and said, 'Look at him! Does he look like a serial killer?' He then ordered Williams to stand up and hold out his hands. 'Look how soft his hands are. Do you think he would have the strength to kill someone, to strangle someone with these hands?' After outbursts like this the prosecution knew that it would be difficult for the jury to envisage the bespectacled defendant as the manipulative, deceitful sexual predator they were portraying unless they could provoke him into revealing his darker side.

At that time profiling was not recognized by the courts as a legitimate tool, so FBI agents from the BSU were not able to testify as to MO or the significance of the signature linking the two murders Williams was charged with to the dozen or more homicides they believed he was responsible for. They were forced to fall back on forensics which included 700 pieces of hair and fibre evidence tying the victims to the defendant's car and home. This should have been sufficient to convict him, but the prosecution's forensic experts talked over the heads of the jury, arguing the significance of data that simply didn't mean anything to the layman. The defence countered with a far less impressive expert but he succeeded in sowing sufficient doubt in the jury's mind regarding the trace evidence to take the edge off the argument. It was at this critical point that Williams played the racist card, accusing the Mississippi police department of both incompetence and ingrained prejudice which succeeded in diverting attention from the scientific evidence and threatened to undermine the entire prosecution case. Fortunately, FBI profiler John Douglas had been in court throughout the trial and by this time had sized up the type of personality they were up against. He told Assistant District Attorney Jack Mallard that Williams had a fatal flaw. He was what is known as a rigid personality, an obsessive-compulsive control freak, who can be riled when put under extreme pressure and his integrity questioned. It was known that Williams had demanded that his lawyers conduct the case according to his instructions. He had even attempted to coach the expert witnesses who had been called to testify on his behalf. If the prosecution could exploit this weakness they had a chance to get him unglued.

When Williams finally took the stand he played the part of the innocent, injured party to perfection. For a full day and a half he protested that he was a fall guy stitched up by a corrupt justice system to divert attention from their failure to apprehend the real killer. When his attorney returned to his seat few would have given odds against an acquittal. Then Jack Mallard was invited to cross-question him. For several hours Mallard kept up the pressure, going over Williams' personal history in minute detail, highlighting inconsistencies in his statements to the police and in his earlier testimony. But Williams held up well, relishing being centre stage and smugly satisfied at his own pitch perfect performance. Then during a lull in the proceedings Mallard leaned in, put his hand on Williams in an intimate gesture of reassurance and disarmed him with a question designed to catch him off guard. 'What was it like, Wayne?' Mallard drawled in his soft southern accent. 'What was it like when you wrapped your fingers round the victim's throat? Did you panic? Did you panic?'

Williams became very still and quiet. 'No,' he said. Then he realized what he had said and flew into a rage. He pointed at Douglas and screamed, 'You're trying your best to make me fit that FBI profile and I'm not going to help you do it!' He spat bile at the prosecution while the jury sat with their mouths wide open and the defence tried vainly to calm their client down, but it was too late. The real Wayne Williams had been unmasked. He was subsequently found guilty and sentenced to two consecutive terms of life imprisonment. To this day he stubbornly maintains his innocence.

In 2004 Williams petitioned the federal court for a retrial on the basis that the police had knowingly ignored evidence of Klan involvement in the killings and on the basis that the forensic evidence was unsound. The appeal dragged on for almost three years before a federal judge dismissed it in October 2006.

Doubts concerning Williams' guilt persist with law enforcement officers and relatives of the child victims weighing in on the side of Williams. A Department of Justice report in 2015 raised questions over the forensic evidence, specifically the emphasis placed on dog hairs which matched Williams' German Shepherd. But prosecutors argued successfully that the hairs played a minor role in the case.

Chapter Five:
Two Minds

'It wasn't as scary as it sounds. I had a lot of fun ... killing somebody's a funny experience.'

Albert DeSalvo, serial killer

Several times during the course of their initial interview with Ed Kemper the agents had to remind themselves that this self-conscious and sensitive guy had been convicted of eight counts of first degree murder and, when asked what his punishment should be replied, 'Death by torture.' But was he crazy? By the end of the session Douglas and Ressler had formed the opinion that killers like Kemper are abnormal but not insane. This distinction is an important one. An offender who is clinically insane will commit a criminal act regardless of the risk to himself, whereas even the most depraved serial killer or sexual predator will have some degree of control regardless of what their lawyer or psychiatrist might later say in their defence. Even the psychopath will restrain himself if he believes he is likely to encounter resistance or be witnessed in the act. Frequently, juvenile offenders will openly defy bystanders to intervene during the commission of a crime, but this is the bravado of antisocial youth. As John Douglas has noted, no serial killer has ever felt so overcome with the compulsion to commit murder that he did so in the presence of a uniformed police officer, a factor known in profiling as the policeman at my elbow principle.

By definition, the insane cannot control their thoughts or their actions, whereas the recidivist rapist and the repeat murderer give in to their impulses when it serves their purposes. Their behaviour is a form of addiction but it is one based on their need to manipulate, dominate and control their victims. To this end many learn how to seduce their prey and evade detection – these are not the acts of an insane person. In jail they may act like model prisoners, but it is just that, an act. Serial offenders and sexual predators curb their desires when they are locked up because they are denied access to their preferred victims, but according to the profilers who have studied them in depth, they cannot be reformed. Many mental health experts agree. A recent study showed that psychopaths were four times more likely to commit a violent offence after release from a therapeutic community than other patients. A former psychopathic patient who attended one of these programmes went so far as to describe it as a finishing school in which he'd learned how to put the squeeze on people.

There Are No Monsters – The Myth That All Killers Are Crazy

When FBI profiler Gregg McCrary expressed his disbelief that a psychopathic killer was due for release from the Atascadero State Hospital in California, the man's doctor explained that, legally speaking, psychopathy is not recognized as a treatable disorder.

The doctor added wryly, 'We only release the really dangerous ones.'

The inherent flaw in the insanity defence was highlighted during the trial of the situational serial killer Arthur Shawcross, who switched from murdering children to preying on prostitutes. The prosecution called in forensic psychiatrist, Dr Park Dietz, to give evidence on the defendant's mental state. Dr Dietz pointed out that, although Shawcross claimed to have eaten parts of his victims and exhibited all the signs of antisocial personality disorder, this did not necessarily reveal the existence of a mental disease or defect which would impair his ability to differentiate between right and wrong, which is the legal definition of insanity. Moreover, Shawcross led an ordered life which a person of unsound mind would not have been able to do. He was married and had a regular job, but the most damning aspect – other than his confession and the fact that he had led police to the bodies of several victims – was his attempt to evade capture. This proved he was capable of reasoning and of understanding that what he had done was wrong.

Dr Dietz added:

'None of the serial killers that I have had the occasion to study or examine has been legally insane, but none has been normal either. They've all been people who've got mental disorders. But despite their mental disorders, which have to do with their sexual interests and their character, they've been people who knew what they were doing, knew what they were doing was wrong, but chose to do it anyway.'

With the matter settled it took the jury just two hours to find Shawcross guilty and sane. He was sentenced to 25 years for each murder. He died at the Albany Medical Center in New York on 10 November 2008 from a heart attack. He was 63.

Incidentally, the Shawcross trial raises another interesting insight into the development of the criminal personality. The profile which the FBI prepared in this case was accurate in all significant respects bar one – the age of the UNSUB. The FBI estimated that the perpetrator would be no older than 30 whereas Shawcross was actually 45 years old. This discrepancy was explained by the fact that an offender's age is relative as his development is effectively suspended during the period of his incarceration. Shawcross had spent 15 years in prison for the murder of two children prior to committing the series of murders for which he was subsequently tried, which made his true age

Arthur Shawcross is formally charged with murder.

about 30, just as the profile had predicted.

Those who advocate the rehabilitation of psychopaths would do well to heed the view of one leading clinical psychiatrist who concluded that such people do not respond to treatment and that the only possible result of educating a psychopath is to produce an educated psychopath.

Profile of a Psychopath

'I just wanted to see how it felt to shoot Grandma.'

Ed Kemper

'Psychopaths, sociopaths and antisocial personalities are different labels for the same psychosis, but they are not the same as psychotic. The psychotic has a serious mental disorder whereas the former three are serious personality problems. It is a sobering fact that one half of one per cent of Americans are estimated to be suffering a form of psychosis*, that is more than one and a quarter million people in a land where gun ownership is a constitutional right and where the police receive on average 400–600 hours training which is one third of that given to beauticians in California.'

Profiles In Murder, Russell Vorpagel and
Joseph Harrington, Dell 1998

The latest research in psychopathology suggests psychopaths are wired differently to the average person, but that such abnormalities can be the result of both genetic and learned behaviour.

A number of recent brain studies seem to prove that psychopaths have inhibited internal connections in their brain which impedes the processing of information. Consequently they exhibit less fear of punishment and constantly search for stimulation to excite their listless nervous system. When antisocial adolescents were shown slides depicting situations which normal individuals would perceive as threatening they produced instead a reduced electrodermal skin response indicative of a subnormal reaction.

In controlled tests these antisocial subjects also failed to read emotional signals as efficiently and accurately as well-balanced individuals. But they over-responded to what are clinically known as distracters, demonstrating a reduced ability to focus, which reveals cognitive deficits in the left hemisphere of the brain. Psychopaths have also been found to lack the ability to differentiate between neutral and emotive words, indicative of an insensitivity to emotional connotations in written and spoken language. Curiously, psychopathic adolescents are more responsive to reward-producing activities than stable subjects and yet they are less deterred by the threat of sanctions or punishment than other subjects.

Early Signs

As children they are likely to express their anger or feelings of inadequacy in aggressive acts towards younger children and small animals. They will despise authority figures and may unconsciously seek attention by setting fires or committing acts of vandalism in locations which symbolize what they perceive to be their places of oppression, specifically their school. But not all will be isolated and withdrawn. Some may project an aura of recklessness which younger children may find attractive. These individuals could attract a small circle of followers who will satisfy their narcissistic need to manipulate and control. To demonstrate their power and influence they may dare another child to commit some act which will then give them a hold over that child.

Canadian analyst Dr David Lykken studied the statistics on juvenile crime and concluded that only a minority of delinquents were born with a predisposition to antisocial behaviour; others either copied from older siblings or adults or were conditioned to regard restraint as a weakness. Lykken suggests that these sociopathic personalities have an uncommonly low fear threshold and a weak behavioural inhibition system which is the direct result of poor parenting, abuse or neglect.

The story of Gary Gilmore is a prime example.

Born Bad?

Gary Gilmore was evidently acutely aware of the danger his compulsion to kill posed to society. After being convicted of murdering two innocent bystanders in cold blood he refused to appeal against his death sentence and expressed his relief at the chance to end his own torment, and silence his inner demons in front of a firing squad in 1977.

Following his death, his younger brother Mikal researched their family history in an attempt to determine whether it was bad blood or background which had sealed his fate. Mikal unearthed a good deal of unsavoury anecdotal evidence in support of the perennial Nurture vs Nature argument. The most pertinent facts were these – Gary's mother and father had been rejected by their own parents and they in turn subjected Gary and his three brothers to a strict religious upbringing, emotional neglect and physical abuse. A fourth sibling had died in infancy.

Their father, Frank Gilmore Snr, was an itinerant conman and alcoholic who allegedly beat his children unmercifully while his wife, Bessie, stood by. When the mood took him he would beat her too and she in turn took it out on the children whom she never tired of telling that the ideal family was one without children. Frank had half a dozen failed marriages behind him, most of which he had simply walked away from without bothering with the inconvenience of divorce.

To sour matters even further Frank got it into his head that Gary wasn't his son, but the product of an earlier liaison Bessie had had, which gave him an excuse to absolve himself of responsibility for the boy. Gary's artistic talents were at first ignored then later repressed, so he exploited the few friendships he made and turned to petty crime.

In time his criminal activities evolved from auto theft to breaking and entering which earned him a spell in reformatory. There he picked up more bad habits and by the age of 16 he had graduated to adult jail. But as soon as he was released, he would commit another offence that would return him to the pen. Gary Gilmore's sole ambition was to die and the bloodier his death, the better, or so he said. A prison psychiatrist diagnosed him as an antisocial personality with intermittent psychotic decompensation. It was only a matter of time before he got his wish.

In July 1976, shortly after being paroled, he shot two men in cold blood on two consecutive nights. As he was strapped down in the chair before the firing squad took up their weapons, his last words were, 'There will always be a father.'

But the fact remains that although the four Gilmore brothers shared the same brutal upbringing only Gary turned to crime. One died of complications sustained in a knife fight, a second simply turned his back on his family and walked away, but Mikal used his experiences as the basis for a book. His telling conclusion was that each of the brothers had dealt with his suffering in his own way. Gary took his rage out on others in a motiveless killing designed to hasten his own end – a not uncommon syndrome the police call suicide by cop. He put no value on the lives of others because he attached none to his own.

Chapter Six:
Bad Seeds and
Women Who Kill

'I wished I could stop, but I could not. I had no other thrill or happiness.'

Dennis Nilsen, serial killer

The struggle against evil was once the mission of the church, but in our more secular age it has become the business of the media to demonize individuals whose acts are so abhorrent as to seem inhuman and to crusade against lenient sentencing for the teenage thugs who batter defenceless old people to death for kicks, the paedophiles who abduct children and the sadistic sex killers who torture their victims for their perverse gratification. All are rightly condemned for their sickening acts of brutality and callous disregard for human life. But it is the murders committed by children for which the more sensation-seeking sections of the media reserve their most righteous indignation.

When Kids Kill

The standard explanation for such crimes is that they are symptomatic of a sick society which glorifies violence and promotes promiscuity, but such rationalizations are simplistic and fail to take into account the backgrounds of these young offenders who will have exhibited aberrant behaviour long before they ever played a violent computer game or were old enough to buy pornographic magazines. Nor does it acknowledge the fact that childish spite, gratuitous cruelty and even wilful murder has been a harsh fact of life long before the invention of games consoles, TV, cinema or even the tabloid press.

In 1786, 12-year-old Hannah Occuish became the youngest female to be executed in the United States having been condemned for the murder of a young girl who she had repeatedly battered with a rock and then strangled out of pure spite.

In 1835, 13-year-old William Wild drowned two toddlers who he later described as floating about like two drowned puppies.

In 1861, two 8-year-old boys, Peter Barratt and John Bradley, were convicted of beating and drowning a toddler in a brook in Stockport, northern England. They were each sentenced to one month in jail to be followed by five years in a reformatory.

In 1872, 12-year-old Jesse Pomeroy was incarcerated for sadistic attacks on four boys who he had whipped, battered and maimed with a knife. Jesse proved to be a model prisoner and two years later was granted an early release upon which he murdered a 9-year-old girl and a 4-year-old boy whom he mutilated almost beyond recognition. He then languished in prison for several years while a successful campaign was waged to persuade the

Governor of Massachusetts to commute his death sentence to life imprisonment. Thirty-eight years later, three psychiatrists and the prison doctor found him well read but unrepentant. He had worked his way through every one of the 8,000 volumes in the prison library and in the process taught himself half a dozen languages as well as the principles of the American justice system. But he remained a cynical, manipulative, self-centred paranoiac. The report concluded:

> *'He takes kindness as a matter of course, is highly egotistical and is inclined to dictate to the prison authorities. His only interest in his mother is the aid she can give him in securing his release. He shows no pleasure at seeing her but begins on his case as soon as she comes and talks of nothing else. He is very unreliable on account of his untruthfulness. He thinks everyone is against him and apparently never loses his suspicions for a moment.'*

Pomeroy was denied parole and died in prison aged 73, a bitter, disgruntled old man.

In 1896, a 9-year-old girl was charged with hacking a 2-year-old to death with an axe after he had bitten her. During the attack she was heard to snarl, 'Ain't dead yet? I'll make you dead.'

And in Providence, Rhode Island, in 1921 a 3-year-old boy put a cord round his playmate's neck, a girl of the same age, looped it round a grindstone and turned the handle. His explanation was disarmingly innocent. 'I don't like her anymore.'

All children are capable of being callous, resentful and wilfully oblivious of the consequences of their actions, but the majority grow out of this egocentric phase when they reach adulthood. However, if guns or knives are readily available in the home, the chance of a tragic accident or worse is greatly increased.

In Florida in 1940 a young boy shot and killed his stepmother because she wouldn't allow him to go to the movies. More recently a spate of High School shootings and drug-related killings by adolescents in the US and Europe has demonstrated that young people are instinctively resorting to weapons to settle their arguments. Many believe that they will get away with it on account of their age. Sometimes they will reach for a gun out of pure vindictiveness.

In Britain a spate of playground stabbings and unprovoked assaults on strangers by teenage gangs are giving the impression that its youth are out of control. It is true that violent crime has been on the increase since the Second World War and this is because we are living in a violence-obsessed society in which social deprivation, overcrowded estates, drug dealing and the availability of weapons are breeding underage criminals faster than rats in a laboratory. In the past the majority of children had the chance to enjoy their childhood before being awoken to the harsh realities of life. Those who are privileged to do so today appear to be in the minority while childhood innocence is under attack from pervasive and harmful influences.

Part of the blame must lie with the more irresponsible sections of the media who are cynically feeding our neurosis. In June 2002 the European Court of Human Rights decreed that politicians would be prohibited from overruling the sentences imposed by judges on young killers in the belief that some might otherwise increase the tariffs to appease the public. In response the *Daily*

Mail, a British tabloid newspaper, published a double-page spread featuring 46 cold-eyed young killers who they would have liked to see locked up for life regardless of the sentences imposed by the courts. The implication was clear. The public have a right to be protected and the judges are too lenient with young thugs. But once we allow career politicians to decide on appropriate punishment, or worse the media, it will be retribution and mob rule which will govern the courts, not justice.

Despite the assertions of the 'hang 'em and flog 'em' lobby it is self-evident that no individual is born evil. That idea belongs to the Middle Ages along with the burning of heretics and witches. Certainly some individuals appear to have been born with a lower capacity for comprehending the consequences of their actions. But invariably the capacity for cruelty has been instilled in them at an impressionable age. When the background of these children is examined, it is almost always the case that they have been desensitized to suffering through years of neglect and abuse and conditioned to believe that violence is an acceptable means of expressing anger. The argument put forward by those who seek retribution rather than rehabilitation is that there are many people who have suffered similar degrees of abuse in the world who have not offended, but child psychologists would say that this is because some people internalize their pain and others externalize it. In fact, those who internalize it are more likely to commit murder because they will have suppressed their rage for longer and so be less able to control themselves when their frustration finally boils over. Some who have suffered deprivation or abuse are psychologically more able to assimilate the experience than others. The case of killer Gary Gilmore who petitioned for his own execution illustrates the point (see page 175). All of the Gilmore children experienced the same brutality from their parents, but only Gary became a murderer. The other brothers dealt with it in their own way. Child psychologists have a theory known as multiple gates which acknowledges that positive and protective factors may come along in time to influence one sibling, but be too late to help another, or one child may be receptive to intervention and another not.

> *'I hated all my life. I hated everybody. When I first grew up and can remember, I was dressed as a girl by mother. And I stayed that way for two or three years. And after that was treated like what I call the dog of the family. I was beaten. I was made to do things that no human being would want to do.'*
>
> Henry Lee Lucas

Vicious Circle

According to Dr Susan Bailey OBE, a British consultant adolescent forensic psychiatrist, children who have experienced deprivation, rejection and disappointment have low self-esteem and no sense of purpose. Instead of blaming the parent or guardian for neglecting or abusing them, they may come to believe that they were ill treated because they were not worthy of love and protection.

They learn that being difficult or violent gives them a sense of power and their provocative behaviour forces adults to pay attention to them. For these children even negative attention is preferable to being ignored. In short, if they can't be loved, they will settle for being feared. That is the lesson they learned from their role models and it will be reinforced by anyone who reacts to their disruptive behaviour with anger and criticism. In cases where the child has been removed from the stressful environment and shown respect, consideration and patience the psychological damage has often been repaired, but as long as the child remains where it feels insecure and vulnerable its own internal self-defence mechanism will maintain an aggressive front and its position will become more entrenched. It cannot afford to lose face by being seen to climb down and turn soft.

Even in the Best Homes...

Contrary to popular belief, deprivation is not confined exclusively to impoverished homes. Emotional neglect can occur even in the most affluent families and often does where the parents are too busy earning a living to give their children the attention they need. The mother of two 15-year-old brothers accused of the murder of 10-year-old Damilola Taylor in south London in November 2000 held down two jobs in an effort to make ends meet, one during the day and another in the evenings, supplementing her income with cleaning jobs which left her hands raw. Neighbours described her as the hardest-working person they had ever known.

But if children are deprived of emotional sustenance and no one shows interest in them other than catering for their material needs, they may grow up lacking empathy and compassion, seeing others as objects instead of as people. But even if their home life is comparatively normal, their school environment may damage them. Bullying by teachers as well as children can marginalize a child as an outsider and can stunt their emotional development, setting that child on the road to a criminal career. Of course, some professional or opportunistic thieves enjoy the thrill and risk of stealing or find it an easy option as opposed to working for a living, and many con artists relish the sense of superiority they get from putting one over on the greedy and the gullible, but serious crimes of violence are almost always committed by individuals who were abused in one way or another in their youth, either at home or at school.

The two brothers, Danny and Ricky Preddie, both of whom had a record for burglaries, were convicted of manslaughter on 9 August 2006 and in October they were sentenced to eight years in youth custody. The uncommonly lenient sentence was justified on the grounds that there was no evidence that the brothers had planned to kill the victim and they had not brought a weapon to the scene. Ricky was released in September 2010 and Danny in 2011. Ricky was subsequently sent back to prison for breaking the terms of his parole.

Gloria Taylor, Damilola's mother, died of a heart attack at the age of 57 in April 2008. Her wish had been to see her son qualify as a doctor.

Graduates of Crime

There appear to be two significant factors determining whether a problem child graduates to more serious offences, specifically violent crime, or continues on the straight and narrow. These are serendipity and fantasy. The former simply means opportunity or bad luck such as in being caught during a robbery or burglary and resorting to violence instead of fleeing the scene. A disturbed, aggressive youth is more likely to take along a weapon and use it instinctively when confronted or cornered, whereas a youth who had simply mixed in with a bad crowd would probably not have even considered carrying a weapon and would flee at the first sign of trouble. Of course, if drugs or alcohol are in the mix even the most passive teenager can become unpredictable.

The latter acknowledges that every child fantasizes about avenging themselves on those they think of as having humiliated or hurt them, but in a normal child their own conscience or parental influence will remind them of the need for restraint.

Children from a secure loving environment know that bad things are ultimately, if not immediately, punished and good deeds will be rewarded, and so will learn to trust that small grievances will be addressed by those in authority, whereas a child starved of affection and attention and conditioned to expect inconsistent responses will have no expectation of their injuries being considered seriously. Their sense of proportion and their perspective is distorted meaning that they will overreact to the slightest provocation, striking out impulsively, taking the law into their own hands as they have no expectation of impartial justice. It is therefore wrong for adults to judge troubled children and teenagers by their own moral code. Adults know that if they can't have something they desire today, they are likely to be able to afford it tomorrow, next week or next month. But a young person who is emotionally immature and inexperienced can only conceive of the here and now.

When they find the present stressful they may retreat into a fantasy world fed by violent images obtained from the internet or from computer games, where they can exert some form of power. A well-adjusted child can distinguish between their fantasy life and reality, but a lonely, disturbed child who is likely to be a low achiever academically may retreat into the world of violent computer games, movies and later sadistic pornography where they imagine meting out retribution and dispensing justice. But these passive activities will not address the issues that feed their frustration. Eventually they may feel compelled to act out these scenarios and, being inadequate types, they will choose victims who are weaker than themselves. This usually means that disturbed boys may grow up to take out their anger on small children or women.

Those who argue that it is nature rather than nurture are often those who view the world in theological terms, as the struggle between Good and Evil. They see child killers as a species, rather

Low-level vandalism can be the first step on the road to serious crime.

than individuals who shared an abusive upbringing which was not addressed in time. Many habitual young offenders have to all intents and purposes regressed to an earlier stage of their development to protect themselves from reality, the egocentric stage where nothing is real unless they can see it for themselves. The suffering of others has no meaning because there are no other people in the world but them, the offender. Like a spiteful, selfish child they want to deprive others of what they can't have so they'll steal it or vandalize it. Many who have been abused suffer from a form of post-traumatic stress disorder and have gone beyond the point where their behaviour can be corrected by punishment. This does not, of course, excuse their behaviour, but it goes some way towards explaining it. Those who have worked with problem children and violent adult offenders have witnessed the result of neglect and abuse. They would say that children are not born evil; the evil is in a system which fails to protect them and in doing so completes the vicious circle.

If proof is required that violence only begets more violence and that killers are made rather than born the case of Mary Bell, one of Britain's most notorious child murderers, supplies all the evidence one would need.

Mary Bell

The first words that Mary heard in this world were, 'Take that thing away from me!' Her mother, Betty, was just 17 and unmarried when Mary was born (in Newcastle on 26 May 1957) and saw the child as an unwanted burden. Her repeated attempts to be rid of her and the abuse she later inflicted on Mary should have alerted the social services, or at least her grandmother with whom she was living at the time, to the danger the child was in.

But there was no law in England at the time to prevent parents from beating their children or sending them to school barefoot or malnourished. And whenever accusations were made both social services and the police were inclined to accept the word of the parents over that of the child. No one in authority pried into what went on behind locked doors unless a child continually came to school with obvious injuries or someone made a formal complaint. Certainly no one intervened in Mary's case until it was too late.

When she was just a year old she was rushed to hospital by her grandmother after swallowing a quantity of pills which were kept out of her reach in a compartment of an old gramophone. The pills were bitter so would not have been mistaken for sweets even if little May, as she was then called, had been able to reach them. But no one remonstrated with her mother. It was not, however, an isolated incident. At the age of three her aunt Cathy saw Mary and her little brother eating the sweets she had bought them earlier that day and noticed that among the Dolly Mixtures were tablets she immediately recognized as Purple Hearts (amphetamines) which Betty had insisted were kept out of harm's way in her handbag. Cathy saved the children from having their stomachs pumped by making them drink salt water until they were sick. Again, Betty blamed Mary for taking her pills, but why would she have done so when she had sweets to eat? Around the same time Mary swallowed a large quantity of iron supplements. This time Betty's protestations of innocence were proven to be false as one of Mary's little friends had seen Betty give them to her and heard her tell Mary that they were sweets. Neurological experts now believe that overdoses of supplements can have a physical effect on the brain which can express itself in behavioural problems. In the case of a child the risk of this occurring is significantly increased. Whether this is true in Mary's case we will never know, but if the repeated intake of pharmaceuticals didn't adversely affect her, it is almost certain that she did suffer psychological damage after seeing a 5-year-old playmate run over and killed by a bus. After these incidents, her behaviour became noticeably disruptive. She broke her uncle's nose by hitting him with a toy and at nursery school she practised strangling other children.

Shortly after the Purple Hearts incident the same uncle saved her from falling to her death from an open window, prompting the family to swear that they would never leave Mary alone with her mother again. It has been suggested that Betty Bell may have suffered from 'Munchausen's Syndrome by Proxy', a psychological disorder which compels people to deliberately put other lives at risk in order to make their own existence more exciting. This could have led her to cause her daughter's accidents in order that she could play the drama queen and the martyr. MSbP can manifest in caregivers who intentionally injure their children or patients in order to elicit the sympathy of others. The typical MSbP mother is unmarried and may feel compelled to give up the child only to demand that they be dramatically reunited. Such an emotional roller-coaster ride would naturally have a traumatic effect on the child's development.

MSbP was not diagnosed until 1977 so Mary's relatives would not have been able to have Betty treated even if they could have persuaded her to seek help. Nor were they able to prevent Betty from marching the child to an adoption agency and foisting her on

A photo of Mary Bell taken inside reform school.

a prospective mother with the words, 'I brought this one in to be adopted. You can have her.' Then she went home. Unfortunately for Mary her aunt Isa traced the woman and dragged Mary back to her mother where, unknown to the rest of the family, she was apparently subjected to unspeakable sexual abuse by a succession of men who paid Betty for sex with her 5-year-old.

Her mother would force the child to give oral sex to these strangers, gripping her hands behind her so she could not wriggle free and pulling her hair back so that Mary would open her mouth. When they were done the child would vomit. While the neighbourhood children were playing hopscotch or ball in the street, Mary would be forced to play Blind Man's Buff with these perverts under the threat of being locked up in a sentry box on the Tyne Bridge.

This constant mental and emotional torture affected her in many ways including making her a chronic bed-wetter to which her mother would respond by rubbing her face in the urine and then hanging the sheet out of the window for the neighbours to see. It is no wonder that Mary grew up to be a manipulative, devious bully and inevitable perhaps that she would come to the attention of the police.

In May 1968, 11-year-old Mary was implicated in a near fatal fall involving her 3-year-old cousin who sustained severe cuts to his head. It was sufficiently serious for the police to investigate, but when the boy refused to say who had pushed him they couldn't take the matter any further. Besides, by this time Mary had a friend, Norma Bell (no relation), who lived next door and always corroborated her version of events whenever the pair was accused of theft or vandalism. But their friendship appears to have faded after both were accused of trying to strangle two younger children they had picked on while playing around a local sandpit. It was only a matter of time before the girls took their bullying too far.

A few weeks later the body of 4-year-old Martin Brown was found in a condemned house by a group of boys who saw Mary and Norma at the scene. Out of a morbid compulsion to put herself centre stage in any tragedy, Mary agreed to bring Martin's aunt the terrible news that he had had an accident, but her behaviour aroused suspicion. She couldn't suppress a broad grin as she asked Martin's cousin if he cried for the boy and whether Martin's mother missed her son. It was clear she was gloating. Four days later she called at the mother's house and asked to see Martin. When told he was dead she replied cheerily, 'Oh, I know he's dead. I wanted to see him in his coffin.'

Mary celebrated her 11th birthday by breaking into and vandalizing a local nursery where she and Norma left four anonymous handwritten notes in a childish scrawl confessing to the murder of Martin Brown. The police dismissed these as a malicious prank, but if they had seen what Mary drew in her school book that same day they might have acted sooner or taken them more seriously.

Under a brief childish description of the events leading to the discovery of the dead boy she had drawn the crime scene exactly as the police had found it with the body correctly positioned and, next to it, an empty bottle of tablets which only an eyewitness or the killer would have seen. The drawing was ignored, as was another telling incident a week later when Mary attacked Norma in the street and screamed that she, Mary, was a murderer. A boy who witnessed her hysterical outburst disregarded it as yet another of Mary's sick fantasies. But when the girls were caught breaking into the nursery a second time, the police were forced to act. They released them into the custody of their parents after charging them and giving them a date to appear at a juvenile court. Had they been able to keep them in custody the second murder might never have occurred.

On 31 July 1968, two months after the killing of Martin Brown, another toddler went missing. His name was Brian Howe. When his 14-year-old sister Pat began a search of the neighbourhood she came across Mary Bell who was sitting on a doorstep near her house, and asked her to help look for him. Mary was more than helpful. She pointed out a derelict area with large slabs of concrete known locally as 'the blocks' where she knew Brian lay dead because, as she later claimed, she wanted to give Pat a shock. But Norma, who had joined them by then, feared discovery and interjected, assuring the boy's sister that Brian never played there as it was too dangerous. It wasn't until 11 pm that the police found his body exactly where Mary had wanted Pat to look. It was evident from the blue tinge to his lips and marks around his throat that he had been strangled. But there were other injuries which led police to suspect that a child might be responsible. A closer examination back at the mortuary revealed cuts to the body which were too tentative for an adult killer to have inflicted. Tufts of the child's hair had been cut by a broken pair of scissors which had been found nearby and there had been an attempt to flay skin from the genitals. Detective Inspector James Dobson later remarked, 'There was a terrible playfulness about it, a terrible gentleness if you like, and somehow the playfulness of it made it more, rather than less, terrifying.' Two days later the autopsy revealed another significant mutilation. A letter M had been scratched into Brian's belly with a razor blade, apparently after he had died. It appeared that the killer had originally inscribed 'N' (for Norma?) and this had been altered to an 'M' (for Mary?), probably by a different culprit.

For more than a week over a thousand children were interviewed, but only two gave the police cause for a second look. 'I did think Norma was peculiar,' Dobson later told investigative journalist, Gitta Sereny. 'I mean, I was inquiring into something pretty awful and little Brian was a child they had all known well, but there she was continually smiling as if it was a huge joke.' After calling on her friend Mary next door, Dobson was struck by the suffocating stillness and the dark oppressive atmosphere made more intimidating by the number of heavy crosses around the walls. 'No feeling of a home whatever, just a shell: very peculiar, no sound, beat-up furniture and very little of it and airless, stuffy, dark you know, on a brilliant summer afternoon.' Mary's mother was away on business when Dobson called, but her stepfather was there and he acted strangely. It later transpired that the couple were claiming single parent allowance and didn't want the benefits people to know Betty had a husband. As for Mary, Dobson found her evasive and deceitful. However, he was forced to accept her explanation of her whereabouts on the day of the murder until he could prove otherwise, but her story was riddled with inconsistencies. 'She appeared to see herself in a sort of cliché scenario of a cops-and-robbers film: nothing surprised her and she admitted nothing.'

It wasn't until the morning of Brian Howe's funeral that Dobson realized he had to act:

'Mary Bell was standing in front of the Howes' house when the coffin was brought out. I was, of course, watching her. And it was when I saw her there that I knew I did not dare risk another day. She stood there, laughing. Laughing and rubbing her hands. I thought, "My God, I've got to bring her in, she'll do another one."'

Predictably each girl blamed the other during their interrogation and cast herself as the innocent bystander. The police trusted that a jury would be able to determine whether one or both of the girls was guilty and so formally charged them with the murder of both boys, to which Mary replied nonchalantly, 'That's all right with me.' Norma reacted violently, vehemently denied her part and threatened to get even with the police.

While on remand Mary's behaviour convinced her psychiatrists and her guards that she was incapable of comprehending the seriousness of the charges levelled against her. She fretted over the possibility that her mother might have to pay a fine and she expressed her belief that Brian would not be missed because he didn't have a mother. His father and sister had cared for him after the parents had separated. But not all the experts were taken in by her wide blue eyes and cherubic face. At her trial psychiatrist Dr Orton stated:

'I've seen a lot of psychopathic children. But I've never met one like Mary: as intelligent, as manipulative, or as dangerous ... I think that this girl must be regarded as suffering from psychopathic personality, demonstrated by a lack of feeling quality to other humans, and a liability to act on impulse and without forethought. She showed no remorse whatsoever, no tears

and no anxiety. She was completely unemotional about the whole affair and merely resentful at her detention. I could see no real criminal motivation.'

And there were the offhand statements she allegedly made while awaiting trial which betrayed a sadistic streak. Mary is said to have grabbed a stray cat and remarked, 'I like hurting little things that can't fight back.' She is also said to have told a policewoman that she would like to be a nurse, '...because then I can stick needles into people. I like hurting people.' But of course, it might all have been childish bravado.

At their trial Mary was unemotional except when shouting at Norma for accusing her of instigating the killings, whereas Norma elicited a certain sympathy by shedding childish tears of contrition and looking apprehensive as the proceedings began.

The prosecution characterized Mary as 'an evil and compelling influence almost like that of the fictional Svengali', whereas Norma was the victim, a simple backward girl of subnormal intelligence. 'In Mary you have a most abnormal child, aggressive, vicious, cruel, incapable of remorse, a girl moreover possessed of a dominating personality, with a somewhat unusual intelligence and a degree of cunning that is almost terrifying.'

Swayed by the image of Mary as the callous demon child and Norma as the ingenuous sidekick, the jury acquitted Norma of manslaughter, but found Mary guilty on grounds of diminished responsibility. She was sentenced to detention for life.

Ironically, the only person who appeared to profit from Mary's incarceration was her mother, who sold her story to the tabloids and, when she had spent her ill-gotten gains, pressed her daughter to write letters and poems to sell to a morbidly fascinated press.

Prison appears to have had a profound effect on Mary who claimed to have suffered more abuse as she languished in an all-male institution before she came under the influence of an enlightened reformer who appears to have fulfilled the role of the father she never had. On her release in 1980 she married and four years later gave birth to a daughter. But there was to be no happy-ever-after ending to the Mary Bell story. In 1998 Mary found herself at the centre of a storm of controversy when she collaborated on an autobiography with author Gitta Sereny. Sereny had earned a formidable reputation for her penetrating interviews with notorious figures, namely Hitler's architect Albert Speer and Concentration Camp Commandant Franz Stangl (see page 52), but Sereny committed the ultimate sin in the eyes of the indignant British press by paying Mary for her story. Mary justified her collaboration by stating that she just wanted to set the record straight and that she wanted her daughter to know the truth. But the public furore that resulted from the disclosure that Mary had been paid for her contribution to the book and the subsequent legal proceedings to ensure her lifelong anonymity ended her daughter's innocence. Sereny believes that Mary experienced a metamorphosis from killer to law-abiding citizen without having undergone any serious psychiatric treatment other than counselling, but this is not supported by her apparent inability to accept responsibility for her part in the murders of the two little boys. Mary still seems to be in denial. Her version of events alternates between both deaths being a tragic accident and her weakness to overcome an unconscious compulsion to kill.

'I'm not angry. It isn't a feeling ... it is a void that comes ... it's an abyss ... it's beyond rage, beyond pain, it's a draining of feeling. I didn't intend to hurt Martin; why should I have? He was just a wee boy who belonged to a family around the corner ...' In her

Gitta Sereny, whose work has shone light on to the dark side of human nature.

mind Norma is equally to blame. In attempting to understand the dynamics of their relationship, she says obliquely, 'The weaker makes the other stronger by being weak.'

Those who suspect that her miraculous rebirth as a devoted mother is all an act, one symptomatic of a sociopath, cite what they see as the melodramatic displays of grief she displays when recalling the alleged abuse she suffered at the hands of her own mother – displays which mimic Betty's melodramatic episodes. And with Betty no longer living (she died in 1994) there is no one to corroborate or refute Mary's allegations. Sereny is not oblivious to this criticism:

> 'Her recovery from these terrible bouts of grief, however, was astoundingly quick, and at first these rapid emotional shifts raised doubts in me. Only one thing overrides them – all the discipline she has created inside herself in order to give her daughter a normal life.'

However, one has to wonder why, if all Mary has claimed is true, she invited Betty to live with her and her daughter in the latter years of her mother's life.

Deadlier than the Male – Women Who Kill

> 'To me, this world is nothing but evil, and my own evil just happened to come out 'cause of the circumstances of what I was doing.'
>
> Aileen Wuornos

Contrary to public perception, Aileen Wuornos was not the first American female serial killer. Multiple murderesses are rare, but they are not unknown and they are certainly not a modern phenomenon.

The Hungarian Countess Elizabeth Bathory (b.1560) is often cited as one of the most sadistic and depraved women in history having been accused of luring up to 200 young girls to her castle where they were tortured to death, although there is no evidence to support the enduring myth that she actually bathed in their blood. The case against Lucrezia Borgia (1480–1519), head of Italy's first crime family who was accused of eliminating her enemies with poison dispensed from a hollow ring is, however, almost certainly without foundation. The New England spinster, Lizzie Borden, was accused – and later acquitted – of murdering her parents with an axe in 1892. No one else was ever tried for the crime.

In 1811 housekeeper Anna Zwanziger was beheaded at Nuremburg, Germany after being found guilty of poisoning her employers' dinner guests because she resented their privileged lives and enjoyed watching them writhe in agony. It appears that she had become embittered at the age of 15 when her guardian forced her into a loveless marriage to an alcoholic solicitor who was twice her age. When he had spent their money, she was left to prostitute herself to feed their children. After his death she was used and abused by a succession of men until she wheedled her way into the home of a judge whose wife she poisoned in the expectation of improving her status, but when he too rejected her she sprinkled arsenic in the salt and sugar jars then left; her last spiteful act being to give the baby a poisoned sweet.

In 1905 French mother of three, Jeanne Weber, murdered two

of her three children before working her way through the infants in Montmartre in the guise of a luckless babysitter. Despite her fatal affect on children mothers continued to employ her to nurse their infants even after doctors had commented on the red marks around the throats of those who had died in her care.

It is thought that she then killed her oldest child so that no one would suspect her if she herself was bereaved. But she was unable to control her compulsion and was caught several times in the act of attempting to strangle children. Incredibly each time she managed to persuade the authorities that there was a perfectly innocent explanation for her actions and she was freed to kill again. But in 1908 she was finally convicted of strangling a boy while his father had struggled vainly to prise her fingers from his neck and was committed to an asylum. Two years later, she was found dead in her cell, her hands clasped tightly round her own throat.

Black Widows and Angels of Death

Female murderers tend to commit their crimes for the same reasons as men – greed or gain, jealousy, revenge, sadistic sexual pleasure and psychosis which covers a variety of delusions including the desire to determine who lives and who dies. But more often than not their methodology can have a distinctive feminine twist.

A 'Black Widow' derives her name from her practice of marrying for money then murdering her husband and, if need be, other family members, in such a way as to make their premature death look like an accident, or a fatal illness. Then she may move on, assuming a new identity so that her fatal trail cannot be traced. However, with recent advances in forensics and more stringent identity checks, such crimes have become extremely rare. In the 1980s devout Christian Velma Barfield (b.1932), a grandmother, confessed to a lifetime of poisonings including former husbands, boyfriends, the elderly people in her care and even her own mother. A hundred years before, the unprepossessing Mary Ann Cotton (1832–1873) disposed of as many as 21 of her relatives using arsenic, thereby depriving Jack the Ripper of the title of Britain's first serial killer. And then there are those, like Celeste Beard, who persuade others to do their dirty work for them. In an echo of Alfred Hitchcock's classic thriller *Strangers On A Train*, Celeste managed to convince another woman, her lesbian lover, to kill her wealthy husband.

The Revenge Killer

'I've run out of options. This is all I have left. What else can I do?'
Ruth Ellis minutes before shooting lover, David Blakely

The old saying that hell hath no fury like a woman scorned sums up the motivation of the revenge killer who will take the life of their own lover in order to deprive a rival of the satisfaction of having stolen them, and having done so will probably murder the rival while they are at it. Ruth Ellis, the last woman to be hanged in Britain, shot her former lover, David Blakely, because she couldn't live with the stigma of being spurned. Some jilted women may even become so deranged as to kill their own children to spite the father. Martha Ann Johnson is just one example. Diane Downs was another. She shot her three children at point blank range, then drove them to the Emergency Room where she pretended they had been targeted by a bushy-haired stranger. Prostitute Aileen Wuornos, however, had a different MO. She killed strangers, stole their cars and pawned their possessions in order to get back at the male species in general.

Cop killer Antoinette Frank is surely unique among female serial killers in that she was on the right side of the law when she committed her crimes – she was a serving officer with the New Orleans police department. But transsexual Leslie Nelson didn't know which side he/she was on until the police tried to take away her babies – namely, a collection of guns including an AK47 with which she shot and killed one officer and severely wounded his brother. Nelson delayed her surrender because she couldn't decide which outfit to wear for her grand entrance before the waiting press, who failed to appreciate the irony of her exit line, 'Ready for my close-up, Mr De Mille?' – a quote from Billy Wilder's satire on Hollywood, *Sunset Boulevard*.

And as another example of life imitating art, if any murderess can qualify as the female Hannibal Lecter it must be Katherine Knight, an Australian housewife who skinned and ate her lover.

Angels of Death

The prime candidate for America's first female serial killer is Jane Toppan (1854–1938) who may have murdered as many as 100 people over a 20-year period, but who only confessed to killing 31. She worked as a private nurse in Cambridge, Massachusetts where she targeted elderly patients who had no surviving relatives who would miss them, or at least none who were likely to enquire as to the circumstances of their death. She might have continued administering lethal doses of morphine undetected had she

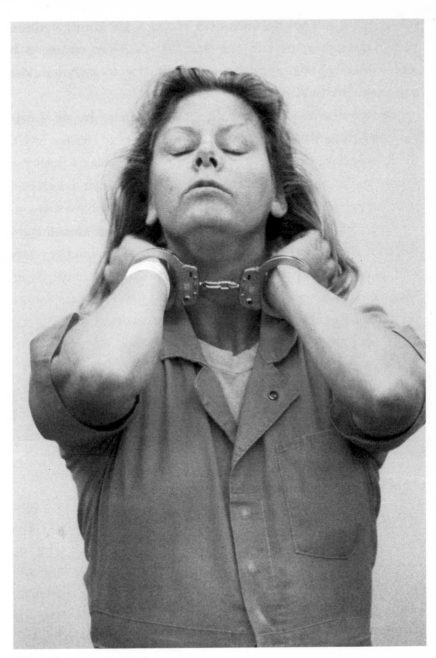

Aileen Wuornos, who killed seven men.

not tried to kill several members of the same family within a suspiciously short period. She fled the scene but was arrested after killing her own stepsister and confined in an asylum in 1901 where she lived until her death at the age of 84.

The women who murder patients under their care are usually suffering from Munchausen's Syndrome by Proxy (see page 190). Such people get a thrill from putting a sick, elderly person or infant at the point of death and then having their relatives or medical personnel witness their frantic efforts to revive them.

American care worker Genene Jones and the British nurse Beverley Allitt are the most notorious baby killers, but the oddest odd couple must surely be Gwen Graham and Catherine Wood who colluded together to murder a number of elderly residents at the Grand Rapids care home in which they worked.

> *'I don't know why I done what I done. The way I done it, I seen it done on TV shows. I had my own way though. Simple and easy. No one could hear them scream.'*
>
> Christine Falling, killer of several infants
> and her elderly employer

The Compliant Partner/Sexual Predator

> *'We had this sexual fantasy see, so we just carried it out. I mean, like it was easy and fun and we really enjoyed it, so why shouldn't we do it?'*
>
> Charlene Gallego

Without doubt the most difficult female offender to understand is the woman who helps procure victims for her male partner to rape, torture and murder. Often these women begin as a compliant victim of a dominant sadistic male (see page 211), but may gradually discover that they enjoy watching their lover abuse another helpless female. In time they may take an active role in the abuse and murder, becoming sexual predators every bit as insatiable and merciless as their partner. Karla Homolka, Charlene Gallego, Myra Hindley and Catherine Birney are just a few of the female serial offenders who exploited their feminine allure to lure other women to their death, while Rosemary and Fred West reversed the roles with Fred procuring the victims for his depraved wife to abuse. Carol Bundy (no relation to serial killer Ted Bundy) was physically unattractive and also seriously disturbed, but was so dependent on her lover Doug Clark that she willingly conspired with him in the killing of young girls so that he would become dependent on her.

Earlier, in the 1940s, the corpulent Martha Beck had indulged in a similar spate of Lonely Hearts killings after teaming up with Raymond Fernandez who murdered single women and widows for their money. More recently, 18-year-old Judith Ann Neeley took the initiative, cajoling her husband into joining her on a killing spree across the southern United States.

Chapter Seven: Sex Crimes

'Killing became the same thing as having sex.'

Henry Lee Lucas

'Killing prostitutes had become an obsession with me. I could not stop myself. It was like a drug ... The women I killed were filth-bastard prostitutes who were littering the streets. I was just cleaning up the place a bit.'

Peter Sutcliffe, the Yorkshire Ripper

What Makes a Serial Rapist?

What makes a man commit rape? Is it more than a lack of self-control? Could there be a biological imbalance in the brain, or does the offender have a compulsion to dominate and humiliate the victim? These questions were among those posed by Dr A. Nicholas Groth, author of *Men Who Rape: The Psychology of the Offender* which became a cornerstone of sexual offender profiling in the US at federal, state and county level during the 1970s.

As he had suspected, Dr Groth concluded that there was no

single, simple answer. He identified four major categories of rapist and two minor categories.

The major categories of rapist are:

Power-reassurance: This is the offender who convinces himself that he has a right to force himself on his victim because he fantasizes that she has agreed to a consensual relationship although she has never said so. He imagines that she has given him non-verbal cues and he won't take no for an answer even when she protests. He is genuinely deluded into believing that she wants him, but he's no less dangerous for that. He may later exhibit guilt and remorse.

Power-assertive: This individual has convinced himself that women exist for his gratification and as such they have no say in the matter. He has no empathy, nor compassion for his victims.

Anger-retaliatory: This offender seeks to degrade and humiliate his victims. He seeks revenge on all women for real or imagined wrongs.

Anger-excitation: The sexual sadist inflicts pain and fear on the object of his anger because he enjoys it. He imagines that he is entitled to hand out retribution because women are innately evil and a threat to his manhood. By dehumanizing them he fantasizes that he is neutralizing their power.

The two minor categories are so called because in these cases rape is not the offender's primary intention. These are:

Opportunistic rapist: He may have been at the scene to commit an unrelated crime such as burglary, but when he finds himself alone with the victim he escalates to rape, usually while under the influence of drugs or alcohol. If he is not caught, he is likely to seek out a similar scenario again, choosing to rob a property owned by a lone female.

Gang rape: In every group that commits this offence there will be a leader and at least one reluctant participant. The latter may become so revolted by what he has been bullied into doing that he turns in the rest. If not, he may be persuaded to give evidence and assist the police once he has been identified as a suspect. The risk of rape escalating into murder is very high with this category of criminal because peer pressure is intense and once they have crossed the line of legality they act instinctively like a pack of wild animals with nothing to lose.

Rape is not always the sexual act it might appear to be. In many cases it is a crime of anger. It is also a fallacy that sadistic sexual offenders are overwhelmed by their desires and act on impulse. Many plan and rehearse their crimes and it is only when their fantasy no longer satisfies them that they decide to make it a reality.

American serial rapist James Mitchell DeBardeleben is a prime example. He demanded that his victims read aloud from a script he had prepared while he tortured them. When he couldn't find a woman to abduct he dressed in female clothing and read the script aloud in a falsetto voice into a tape recorder so that he could get a thrill imagining what it would feel like when he had a real victim at his mercy.

'I made my fantasy life more powerful than my real one ... I carried it too far, that's for sure.'

Jeffrey Dahmer

Sex Slaves

Anyone can become a victim. Many women reassure themselves that they would never fall for the charms of a manipulative man, that they would recognize the danger signs long before they became involved with a sexual sadist, but a study of sadistic sexual predators by the FBI Behavioral Science Unit led by Special Agent Roy Hazelwood revealed that any woman could fit the profile of potential victim.

Sexual sadists do not usually exhibit any outward signs of abnormality. They are usually middle class and pride themselves on their appearance. Their aim is to appear as normal and unthreatening as possible. It is rare for these offenders to have a history of drug or alcohol abuse or a criminal record of any kind. They will have cultivated a veneer of respectability so that their potential victims will have no reason to suspect the darker side of their nature. But these are men who deliberately seek out vulnerable women and are practised in the art of manipulation. They know how to ensnare their victims with gifts, attention and

Jeffrey Dahmer killed 16 young men.

affection which they know these lonely women are craving. Maybe the target is divorced or has ended a long-term relationship. Whatever the case, he seeks them out and exploits that need for companionship and security. Once he is assured of the woman's affection he will gradually isolate her from her friends and family so that she will become dependent on him both emotionally and for everything else.

In one particular instance the man persuaded the woman to stop having lunch with her colleagues on the pretext that they needed to save money so they could afford to set up home together. Once he saw she would agree to that he upped the stakes by insisting that she cut down on phone calls to her family.

A typical manipulator may then go on to persuade the woman to alter her appearance and perform sexual acts which will lower her self-esteem, making her feel that they share a guilty secret she would be ashamed for her friends to know about. Now he effectively has something on her, something he can use as leverage. And despite being wracked by guilt and a growing unease she will continue to do what he asks because she wants to please him. But she is also becoming afraid that he might tire of her and withdraw his affections, which she now believes she can't do without.

She is now completely vulnerable and he can degrade her with physical, verbal and sexual abuse so that she is totally devoid of self-respect. Ultimately, he can get her to do anything, even become an accomplice to murder if he wishes it. Once that line is crossed she is more than his slave, her life is in his hands.

The Ken and Barbie Killers

With their blond hair, good looks and toned country club physiques Paul and Karla Bernardo looked every inch the all-American couple. Friends called them Ken and Barbie because of their resemblance to the idealized children's dolls of the same name, but there was nothing cute and cuddly about this couple. Under this facade they were among the most depraved and sadistic killers the FBI had ever hunted. Although Karla's lawyers were later to claim that she was a battered wife and an unwilling accomplice to the crimes, videotapes shot by the couple recording the torture and murder of their young female victims revealed that she was an active and enthusiastic participant. One of those victims was Karla's own 15-year-old sister, Tammy Lyn, whose ordeal Paul enjoyed re-enacting after her death with Karla dressed in her dead sister's clothes.

Paul Bernardo's criminal career had begun in 1987 with a series of vicious rapes in Toronto, Canada and then escalated into kidnap, torture and murder after he had moved across the border to New York State and found an accomplice and a place where he could hold his captives. The change in his personal circumstances and his move to the States had misled the authorities into believing that they were looking for two perpetrators. And yet, both profiles proved to be uncannily accurate.

Out of the Shadows

In the autumn of 1988, FBI agents Gregg McCrary and partner John Douglas received a bulging case file containing details of seven unsolved violent sexual offences and were asked to provide a profile which would help catch the perpetrator. Six of the assaults had occurred in Scarborough, a suburb of Toronto, and the seventh in Mississauga, a neighbouring city to the south-west.

In all but one instance the young women had been followed home from a nearby bus stop, grabbed from behind and dragged into a dark alley where they were assaulted. The seventh had been attacked from the front but even so, she was unable to add to the brief description given by the other victims. All agreed the man was white, in his late teens or early twenties, of athletic build, approximately 6 ft (1.8 m) tall with light brown or blond hair and good-looking. He was clean-shaven and had no discernible accent. The only distinguishing feature was a mole under his nose.

During the first two attacks in May and July of 1987 he had limited himself to fondling and vulgarities, but in December he repeatedly raped a 15-year-old girl at knifepoint and forced her to repeat profanities that aroused him while he tightened a cable around her neck. This latest attack had occurred in a more densely populated area and was an indication that the offender's confidence was increasing. Two days before Christmas a 22-year-old woman was subjected to the same ordeal then left with a vicious kick in the ribs. Bravely, she ignored his departing threat not to go to the police and was able to add to the description of the assailant. This was sufficient to have an artist's sketch made, but for reasons that were never revealed the police decided not to circulate it. Then the rapist went to ground.

For several months there were no further reported incidents until April 1988 when another young woman was raped by a man who subdued her from behind and ordered her to repeat his lewd script, but this attack occurred miles away in Mississauga. Could this have been the work of the same offender? Investigators decided it was likely to be as the core behaviour was essentially the same. Again, he had demanded that his terrified victim humiliate herself by repeating every profanity he could think of. The same month he struck again, assuming it was the same man, but this time back in Scarborough. In retrospect the pattern seems clear, but the Toronto Sexual Assault Squad are asked to investigate on average 1,500 rapes each year and nothing could be stated with certainty. Nevertheless, female officers were assigned as decoys to ride likely bus routes in the hope of luring this sadistic serial rapist out of the shadows. But there were no firm leads. And the attacks were increasing in brutality. The sixth victim had her collarbone broken in the struggle and had dirt rubbed into her hair and body. In desperation the Toronto police sent the files to the BSU.

Scouting the Scene

In the company of two local officers, FBI profilers Douglas and McCrary surveyed the crime scenes in the gathering dusk to familiarize themselves with the neighbourhood as the victim and UNSUB had seen it on the nights of the attacks. The first thing McCrary noted was that Scarborough was an upper-middle-class community. If the offender lived there and he was in his early twenties it was unlikely that he could have afforded a home of his own. It was almost certain that he would be living with his parents. And anyone with such a pathological hatred of women would not have been able to keep their feelings to themselves. In moments of extreme agitation he must have blurted out something that would have betrayed his true nature and incriminate him.

They could rule out an outsider who might have chosen the victims in town and rode with them on the bus into the suburbs for the simple reason that there would not have been a cluster of crime scenes in Scarborough if that was the case. He had to be a local man, stalking his prey in his own backyard, his comfort zone, specifically within walking distance of the first, second and fifth attacks. This would explain why he attacked the women from the rear. They may have recognized him had they seen him approaching. It is revealing that the Mississauga victim was assaulted from the front indicating that he had no fear of being recognized being so far from home. The trick was to catch him before he grew confident enough to hunt further afield. The ritualistic repetition of a script, specifically the words that fuelled his fantasies of being a better lover than the victim's current boyfriend, revealed that he harboured inadequacies and needed constant reassurance that he was superior to both these women and other men. But he only chose young petite defenceless women who he could be sure of subduing.

The streets of Scarborough were densely populated, neat rows of houses with one or more cars parked in the driveway, the odd boat on a trailer and well-maintained shrubs, hedges and fences where a predator could take cover. A steady stream of traffic in the early evening suggested that the perpetrator was willing to take risks and probably derived an added thrill from the thought that he could be caught in the act. There is a theory currently circulating among mental health professionals that psychopaths have an underdeveloped nervous system which requires constant stimulation in order for them to feel alive, but there is no physical evidence to support it. The excessive use of force in the absence of resistance indicated that the UNSUB must be a psychopath which meant that his hatred of women would not be satiated by rape alone. It was clear from the escalating violence exhibited in the attacks that his rage was boiling over. It was only a matter of time before he graduated to murder.

The Scarborough Rapist

The following extract from the official FBI report into the Scarborough rapes reveals the level of detail profilers are required to provide to law enforcement agencies. The report was submitted to the Metropolitan Toronto Police on 17 November 1988. After a summary of the assaults and an assessment of the victims Special Agents Gregg McCrary and SSA James A. Wright offered their analysis of the offender.

'*We do not believe the offender would attack a victim with a premeditated idea of murdering her. However, we would opine, based upon our research and experience, that if confronted by a victim who vigorously resists his attack, your offender is the type who would likely become so enraged he could lose control and thereby become capable of unintentionally murdering the victim.*

This type of behaviour is observable in your offender to a lesser degree in these attacks. In analysing the interaction between the individual victims and the offender it can be seen that the victims feel overpowered by him and are generally compliant and submissive. Still, when the victims either misunderstand a command or delay, even momentarily responding to a demand, the offender immediately becomes enraged and escalates the amount of violence directed at the victim.

The offender's escalation in violence is observable also as the first three attacks could be seen as attempted rapes where no penile penetration occurred, while the rest of the attacks were successful rapes from the offender's view point as he achieved penile penetration. This expansion of the sexual nature of the assaults was accompanied by an escalation in the verbal and physical violence directed at the victims.

Also observable in the offender is the development of sadistic tendencies. He asked the seventh victim, should I kill you, thereby making her beg for her life. The sadist achieves gratification by the victim's response to his attempts to dominate and control her either physically or psychologically, by posing a question that made the victim beg for her life he is deriving pleasure.

He has shown adaptive behaviour, indicating he is becoming comfortable in committing the assaults and feels unthreatened and in control. This is exemplified in the sixth attack. While he was accosting the victim and attempting to gain control over her, a car pulls out of a driveway a few inches away and drives by them. He does not panic, but forces the victim into some bushes near a house and continues to assault her.

Offender Characteristics and Traits:
Your offender is a white male, 18 to 25 years of age. It should be cautioned that age is a difficult category to profile since an individual's behaviour is influenced by emotional and mental maturity, and not chronological age. No suspect should be eliminated based on age alone. The behaviour exhibited throughout these assaults suggests a youthful offender rather than an older more mature one.

As noted above, we believe your offender lives in the Scarborough area. He is familiar with Scarborough, especially the initial assault sites, and, therefore, in all probability lives in the immediate vicinity of those first assaults.

The offender's anger towards women will be known by those individuals who are close to him. He will speak disparagingly of women in general conversation with associates.

He had a major problem with women immediately before the onset of these attacks. His anger would have been apparent not only for the particular woman involved but those close to him.

He is sexually experienced but his past relationships with women have been stormy and have ended badly. In all probability he has battered women he has been involved with in the past. He places the blame for all his failures on women.

If he has a criminal record, it will be one of assaultive behaviour. The arrests will likely be for assault, disturbing the peace, resisting arrest, domestic disturbance, etc.

His aggressive behaviour would have surfaced during adolescence. His education background will be at the high school level with a record of discipline problems. He may have received counselling for his inability to get along with others, his aggressiveness, and/or substance abuse.

He is bright, but an underachiever in a formal academic setting.

He is nocturnal and spends a good deal of time on foot in the target assault area.

We believe your offender is single.

The offender has an explosive temper and can easily become enraged. This rage transfers over into the rest of his life.

He blames everyone else for his problems.

His work record will be sporadic and spotty as he cannot hold a job due to his inability to handle authority.

He is financially supported by his mother or other dominant female in his life.

He is a lone wolf type of person. He can deal with people on a superficial level but prefers to be alone.

The personal property of the victims which your offender took from the assault scenes is being kept by him. These effects are viewed as trophies by the offender and allow him to relive the assaults. He will keep these items in an area which is under his personal control which he feels is secure, but yet allows him ready access to them.

The nature of these attacks will continue to be episodic and sporadic. In all probability, they will continue to occur outdoors as he is familiar with the area and this familiarity gives him a sense of freedom and mobility which would be denied if he were to attack indoors. Each attack is precipitated by a stressor in the offender's life. This stressor could be either one in fact or in his mind.

The offender recognizes his inadequacies and attempts to mask them, but very often overcompensates. These inadequacies are not known by casual acquaintances, but are well known by those closest to him.

POST OFFENSE BEHAVIOUR:
Your offender harbours no guilt or remorse for these crimes. He believes his anger is justified and, therefore, so are the resultant attacks. His only concern is being identified and apprehended.

Any further questions regarding this analysis or discussion regarding investigative strategy and interview techniques should be directed to SA Gregg O. McCrary or SSA James A. Wright, F.B.I. Academy, Behavioral Science Unit.'

The Killings Begin

During his tenure in the BSU, Special Agent Gregg McCrary had pinned a cartoon to his office bulletin board depicting a dragon standing over the prostrate body of a defeated knight. The caption read, 'Sometimes the dragon wins'. In the summer of 1991 it looked as if the dragon was having it all his own way. The Scarborough rapist had chalked up 15 victims and had still not been caught, while in the neighbouring region bordering New York State, known locally as the Golden Horseshoe, a series of abductions of young girls was causing the Niagara Regional Police serious concern.

Fourteen-year-old Leslie Mahaffy was the first to go missing. On 15 June she had returned home late with a male friend to find the house dark. After banging in vain on the locked doors, her friend left for home assuming that Leslie would find a place to sleep. It was the last time he saw her alive. Her dismembered body was found two weeks later 30 miles (48 km) east on the shore of Lake Gibson in eight concrete blocks. She had been sexually assaulted then dismembered with a chainsaw.

While forensic experts examined the blocks and body parts for trace evidence, detectives began to draw significant clues from the means in which the body had been disposed. It only took a sharp blow with a pick to split the concrete blocks apart which suggested that the killer was an amateur handyman. He had evidently made the blocks in two stages and had allowed the first half to set before pouring in the second to seal it. This meant that the bond between the two halves was easily broken. If he had been in the building trade in any capacity he would have known the correct way to pour cement. His choice of a chainsaw was the second significant clue. It is a messy and inefficient method of dismembering a corpse, suggesting that he had a limited number of tools to choose from. The noise would also have alerted neighbours so he must have had the privacy of a workshop where he could work without fear of being disturbed and where he could clean up afterwards, erasing every trace of her presence. So it was a fair assumption that he was employed in a semi-skilled capacity and was familiar with tools. The location of the body parts was also significant. It betrayed his lack of local knowledge. Anyone living in the area would have known that the lake was routinely drained and so would have chosen a spot further upstream. But he was obviously aware that the dump site was near a lovers' lane, so it was possible that he had recently moved to the area and was only familiar with the obvious landmarks. Manhandling eight concrete blocks would have required some help, so it was almost certain that he had an accomplice and if he had wanted to avoid arousing attention in a lovers' lane it was likely his accomplice was a woman.

A second murder occurred on 10 August when the body of 18-year-old Nina de Villiers was discovered naked in a creek which sparked rumours that a serial killer was at large in the region, but her murderer was eventually identified and his hair was different to that found in the concrete blocks containing the first victim.

And then on 30 April, the naked body of 15-year-old Kristen French was discovered in Burlington two weeks after her abduction, half a mile from her home in St Catherines. It was covered with leaves and branches. Her hair had been cut short and it was clear from bruising to her face that she had been brutalized before being strangled. The body had been washed before being dumped and the state of decomposition indicated that she had been kept alive for two weeks before she was murdered.

At first glance the killings appeared to be unconnected. Leslie Mahaffy had been dismembered. Kristen French had not. Mahaffy had been buried in concrete and dropped in a lake, French was found out in the open partially hidden by leaves. Mahaffy had disappeared at night, French was abducted in daylight. And yet, the girls were of a similar age, they had both been sexually assaulted and apparently asphyxiated. Furthermore, both had almost identical indentations on either side of the spine where the killer had presumably knelt on their backs to exert pressure when strangling or suffocating the girls from behind. But what nagged at Agent McCrary as he crossed the border into Canada to assist the Niagara Police, was that the first girl had been abducted in Burlington and dumped in St Catherines, whereas the second victim had been abducted in St Catherines and her lifeless body dumped in Burlington. Moreover, Kristen had been left just yards from the cemetery where Mahaffy had been buried. Could it be that the killer(s) had stopped at the grave before or after dumping the body?

On arrival in Toronto McCrary found feelings running high and patience wearing thin. The kidnapping and killing of the two young girls together with two others in the same period which, at the time, were thought to be part of the series, had the local press baying for blood. The local police were doing all they could with limited resources, but unknown to them, they were following false leads given by well-meaning but mistaken eyewitnesses. Several conscientious citizens recalled seeing two men cruising the neighbourhood where Kristen had been kidnapped in a cream-coloured Camaro. They even described rust spots and evidence of crude repair work on the driver's door. Valuable man hours were wasted on this line of inquiry as officers checked dozens of auto-repair shops, dealers and gas stations to eliminate all but one of the 125,000 Camaros registered in Ontario. But nothing of potential value could afford to be disregarded.

In an effort to stir things up the *Toronto Star* offered a reward of $100,000 to anyone offering information that would lead to a conviction and a local TV station broadcast a 90-minute special in the hope of focusing public attention on the case. It featured an interview with Agent McCrary, who offered a sketch of the killer based on the profile he had prepared for the Toronto police.

He identified the crimes as high-risk, sexually motivated stranger homicides which are generally committed by men with a well-developed fantasy life which compels them to take greater risks and increases the chance of them making mistakes. Such men often begin with lewd behaviour and obscene phone calls, before escalating to sexual assault, then rape and ultimately sadistic sexual murder. But although they are constantly on the prowl for potential victims, they will not act to fulfil their fantasy unless presented with an opportunity that is too good to miss or are pushed over the edge by a stressor – such as a fight with their partner.

When there are two offenders acting together, one will be the dominant personality and the other subservient. In such cases it is the dominant partner who will be profiled as it is his fantasy which is manifested in the crime. In this case the offender was a predatory psychopath who hated women and enjoyed inflicting pain. If he had a female partner he would be abusive to her too, but if she questioned his authority he would feel compelled to find a victim over whom he could exercise his need to control.

McCrary ended on a note that was intended to drive a wedge between the offender and his accomplice. He expressed the opinion that the latter was likely to be feeling guilty over their part in the murders as they probably hadn't intended the abductions to end that way. This was intended to give the submissive partner the idea that he or she would have a sympathetic hearing if they gave themselves up and assisted the police, giving them the idea that there might be the chance of a reduced sentence if they intervened before another killing could take place. But McCrary also hinted that time was running out. They would both be caught eventually and if the dominant partner believed that his accomplice knew too much, he may silence him or her to keep them from testifying.

Although he did not say so on screen, McCrary was almost certain that the Scarborough rapes and the murders of the two girls had been carried out by the same party, or parties. As it turned out, both offenders were sexual sadists and these account for less than two per cent of all sexually violent offenders. The chance of two individuals of their type operating in such a small area was remote to say the least.

Fatal Attraction

The break in the case came just over six months later on 5 January 1993 when the St Catherines police received a call from the local hospital informing them of a serious domestic assault: 23-year-old Karla Homolka had been brutally beaten with a flashlight by her husband and had decided to file charges. His name was Paul Bernardo. The divide and conquer strategy had evidently worked but it had taken time: the idea had preyed on Karla's mind, but her husband had exercised such control over her that it had taken another bout of physical abuse before she had finally been forced to break cover and seek help. The authorities had been looking for two men, but that was understandable. Sexual predators rarely work in pairs and when they do it is invariably two males. The witnesses had not had a clear sighting of the second offender in the passenger seat of the car. The car, too, had been wrongly identified. It was not a yellow or beige Camaro, but a gold Nissan.

The error had not only cost valuable man hours in following a false trail, but it had probably dissuaded a friend, work colleague or neighbour of Bernardo's from relaying their suspicions to the police because Bernardo drove a different car.

Bernardo not only fitted the profile compiled for the killer of Leslie Mahaffy and Kristen French, but also the earlier profile McCrary had created for the Scarborough rapist. But this was only brought to light when DNA samples taken back in November 1990 were finally processed and identified as being the same as those recovered from the crime scenes. Incredibly, it had taken more than two years for forensic scientists to work their way through the 224 samples taken during the Scarborough rape investigation and eliminate all but one. In the real world that is the time it takes to conduct a thorough analysis in the lab. It is only on TV shows such as *CSI* that the results spill out of the computer before the tecs have finished their coffee.

It appeared that the rapes had stopped because Bernardo had moved from Scarborough – where he had been living with his parents as the initial profile had predicted – to Port Dalhousie where he had committed another rape before graduating to abduction and murder.

But the DNA only proved that Bernardo was guilty of the rapes. It did not link him to the murders. For that the police would need a confession from Karla testifying to her husband's part in the torture and murder of the two young girls.

Inexperienced officers might have confronted Karla with the circumstantial evidence and risked her clamming up to avoid implicating herself in the crimes. Instead the local police arrived at her aunt and uncle's house where she had taken refuge from her husband and interviewed her about the domestic assault.

This opened a dialogue with the officers and lulled her into a false sense of security. Then the investigators from the Toronto Sexual Assault Squad identified themselves and implied that the couple might know something about the Scarborough rapes and might also have been in the vicinity when Kristen French had been kidnapped. But no accusations were made.

When they left the apartment Karla broke down and confessed all to her aunt and uncle who advised her to find a lawyer. This played right into the hands of the police who knew that a smart attorney would have Karla's interest at heart, not her husband's. A deal was cut with the Canadian Ministry of Justice in July 1993 giving Karla complete immunity from prosecution in exchange for a full confession.

But it was only after the deal was struck that the true extent of her part in the murders came to light.

Incriminating Evidence

The police undertook an extensive search of the couple's rented house in Port Dalhousie from where they recovered sufficient forensic evidence for a prosecution, but they had failed to find the stack of video tapes that Karla claimed Paul had made of the murders. McCrary was certain they were in the house. He knew that men like Bernardo could not bring themselves to part with their trophies and that if such tapes could be found they would condemn Bernardo in the eyes of the jury who would see what a callous and sadistic killer he was. But it was not until 15 months later, in September 1994, that a number of incriminating tapes were handed over to the Crown attorneys by Bernardo's own

Karla Homolka, described as a 'deviant personality'.

lawyer. They had been recovered from a secret hiding place in the house by his predecessor, the attorney who had been acting for Paul at the time of his arrest. They were hidden behind a light in a false ceiling and found with the aid of a diagram drawn by Bernardo, who had ordered the attorney to enter the house to recover his personal effects. Incredibly, the police had permitted the lawyer to enter the property unsupervised. As McCrary had predicted, the tapes revealed the full horror of the crimes the couple had committed and the part each had played. Karla had filmed at least one of the Scarborough rapes, so she was clearly more than a battered wife bullied into tagging along. But there was more. The films revealed that Leslie Muhaffy and Kristen French were not the couple's first victims.

Murder at Christmas

At Christmas 1990, Paul Bernardo had left his parents' home in Scarborough and was living with Karla's parents, secure in the belief that he had committed as many as 15 sexual assaults and got away with it. He had even donated DNA when asked for a sample as part of the routine inquiry and had heard nothing since. He must have thought of himself as invincible.

While other couples were exchanging traditional gifts, Karla had something else in mind. She would help Paul rape her 15-year-old sister Tammy Lyn. Paul had made no secret of the fact that he wanted to have sex with Tammy. Karla had even pretended to be her sister when they made love on Tammy's bed while they were alone in the house, but that didn't satisfy Paul. So, after the Homolkas had retired to bed one night, they drugged the girl with Halcion and Halothane stolen from the veterinary clinic where Karla worked, then filmed the rape using a camcorder. The footage also captured Karla's sexual assault on her own unconscious sister urged on by Paul. Things took a turn for the worse when the unconscious girl made a choking sound, vomited and lay still. They dragged her down the hall into Karla's bedroom, dressed her and tried to revive her, but it was clear that Tammy Lyn was dead. When the paramedics arrived they noted a severe burn from the girl's mouth down her neck, indicative of a drugs overdose, but Paul and Karla assured the medics that no drugs were involved. It was a tragic accident, they said – presumably the result of intoxication. The police could not prove otherwise as Karla had washed the bed clothes the moment she heard from the hospital that her sister had been pronounced dead on arrival. At the autopsy, the pathologist could find no trace of foul play and certified her death as accidental caused by choking on her own vomit.

The couple had got away with murder.

Profile of a Sexual Sadist

'I always had the desire to inflict pain on others and to have others inflict pain on me. I always seemed to enjoy everything that hurt. The desire to inflict pain – that is all that is uppermost.'

Albert Fish

Paul Bernardo was an archetypal sexual sadist. He had above-average intelligence – proven by the fact that he had completed a four-year university degree course in three years – but his home life had instilled in him the belief that sexual gratification was

Sadist and killer Albert Fish at 65 years old.

paramount. He was the product of his mother's extramarital affair and was haunted by the idea that his father had been arrested for allegedly abusing his sister. He took a pride in his appearance and was perceived by friends and neighbours as pleasant and polite, but it was a facade. Several former girlfriends described him as generous and considerate, but when he was assured of their affection he would become verbally and physically abusive. One girl noted that he was only aroused when inflicting pain or making her fear for her life – the tell-tale signs of a sexual sadist. But his need to dominate, control and humiliate continued into their daily life. For these men violence has become eroticized. Their ultimate fantasy is to possess another person completely which means having the power of life and death over them. The act of murder is the fulfilment of that fantasy. The fact that it also eliminates a witness is secondary.

Paul had groomed Karla to fulfil his fantasy, but it seems she shared his sadistic urges and, instead of killing her, she became his accomplice in acts of increasing savagery.

Fatal Attraction

They had met when she was just 17 and he was 23. During her initial confession in July 1993, which took a full five days to record, she described how Paul had isolated her from her family and insisted that she dressed in the clothes he chose for her. She even had her hair styled according to his taste. He countered every objection with compliments that overcame her resistance, but his interest in her was self-gratification. He cared nothing for her feelings. He was obsessed with transforming her into his fantasy woman. She was an object to be used and abused. He was devoid of empathy and enjoyed humiliating her, but her willing compliance only made her even less of a human being in his mind. He was contemptuous of her and at the same time aware that she depended on him. It appeared to be a classic case of an abused, submissive partner identifying with her abuser. But Karla was self-assured and had not been denied access to her family by her husband as she had claimed. Could it be that she had simply studied the profile of such couples in one of the stack of true crime books that were found in their house and had memorized the signs in anticipation of her arrest?

The police suspected that Karla had rehearsed her role as she expressed no sense of remorse nor betrayed any signs of guilt. She exhibited none of the characteristics of a compliant victim although she knew how to give that impression. But there was nothing the authorities could do. The deal was watertight. The best they could do was wring her dry for information that would lead to Paul's conviction.

The day of Tammy's funeral, the couple made a sex tape in which Karla dressed in her dead sister's clothes and could be heard promising to lure more young girls for her lover's pleasure. The look of surprise on her husband's face when she said this suggested that it was not part of the script. Just as damning was the excerpt showing Kristen French begging for her life and screaming for Karla to help her, while Karla held the camcorder steady on her husband who was raping and tormenting the girl. Moments later the screen went blank. Kristen was dead.

In May 1995 Paul Bernardo was found guilty on two counts of first degree murder, two counts of kidnapping, two counts of sexual assault, two counts of forcible confinement and one count of committing an indignity to a human body. He was sentenced to life in prison with eligibility for parole in 2020.

At her trial Karla pleaded guilty to two counts of manslaughter as had been agreed and was sentenced to two consecutive ten-year terms with an additional two years for her part in her sister's death. She boasted that she would be out in four years, but at her parole hearing in 1997 it was decided that she was too dangerous to be released. She was denied parole again in 2001. As Agent McCrary commented in his summary of the case, the fact that she could kill her own sister and then continue to participate in more rapes and murders revealed a truly deviant personality.

Following Karla's confession, Tammy Lyn's body was exhumed and examined to determine the true cause of death. It was determined that she had been drugged and raped. When the medical examiner had opened the casket he had found two handwritten notes from Paul and Karla apologizing for their part in her death. It was the only expression of remorse they are believed to have made for any of their victims.

Following Bernardo's conviction, an official report criticized police procedure and concluded that Bernardo had evaded detection due to a lack of co-ordination, co-operation and communication between Ontario's police and other departments in the justice system. As a result of its recommendations, a computerized case management system has been established in the province to serve as a central source of information in all homicide and sexual assault cases. It is the only one of its kind in the world. Bernardo, who was moved to the segregation unit of Millhaven Institution in September 2013, is not eligible to apply for full parole until February 2018, but it is unlikely to be granted due to his 'dangerous offender' status. This appraisal appeared to be confirmed by his uncommonly high score (35/40) on the Psychopathy Checklist which bizarrely pays royalties on its licensed use to its originator, Canadian psychologist Robert D. Hare.

Bernardo used his time behind bars to write a violent conspiracy thriller, *A MAD World Order*, which became a self-published bestselling ebook on Amazon in November 2015 until it was removed from the site after a flood of complaints.

FBI Profiler: Roy Hazelwood

Former FBI agent Roy Hazelwood is regarded as the world's foremost authority on aberrant sexual offences. He spent more than 16 years both studying and solving violent sex crimes as a leading member of the original profiling team based at Quantico, Virginia. Since his retirement in 1994, he has been involved in the founding of a private forensic consulting company, The Academy Group Inc., with former members of the BSU. Roy and his colleagues were credited as consultants on the cult serial killer series, *Millennium*, dreamt up by *X Files* creator Chris Carter, who based his shadowy Millennium Group on Hazelwood's organization.

Roy's interest in serial sex offenders began during his service in the Army Military Police Corps where he attained the rank of major. During basic training he attended a presentation which featured the case of Harvey Glatman, one of the first modern sexual predators to keep their victims in captivity. Glatman was dubbed the Lonely Hearts Killer because he lured his young female victims through advertisements in the personal column of the local newspaper. Once he had them alone he would threaten to kill them if they struggled. Then he would tie them up and take photographs before and after he murdered them. Fortunately, his fourth intended victim managed to free herself and take his gun, turning it on him and threatening to shoot him if he tried to escape. Incredibly, she kept her nerve until the police arrived to arrest him.

After the lecture Roy asked the instructor why Glatman hadn't destroyed the incriminating pictures and was told such things were not important. The suspect had been caught and the girl freed. That was all he needed to know. Dissatisfied, Roy decided that he was going to discover why serial offenders exhibited a pattern of behaviour and if it was possible to use this information to identify and trap them.

On leaving the army, Roy joined the FBI and was assigned to the Academy at Quantico to teach trainee agents how to investigate sex crimes. When he joined the BSU a year later in January 1977, the new soft science of profiling was still being formulated. In fact, Roy's own training consisted largely of long conversations with Howard Teten, a pioneer of profiling, who generously shared his experiences which Roy then passed on to his own students, some of whom were law enforcement officers from out of state.

The profiling programme developed in fits and starts in after-class sessions when these men introduced their own unsolved cases as examples of cases they couldn't crack. Initially the sketchy traits and characteristics Roy and his colleagues were able to offer were sufficient to kick-start the case, but as their reputation grew and word of the uncanny accuracy of the Behavioral Science boys at Quantico spread through the law enforcement community, they began to receive requests from all over the country asking for more detailed profiles, many of which were accompanied by a wad of crime scene photos and a bulging case file. Not surprisingly perhaps, Larry Monroe, the unit chief, wasn't too happy about the amount of time Roy and the other teachers were investing in their extra-curricular activities and assigned John Douglas to co-ordinate them, Howard Teten having moved on. In 1979, Monroe decided that anyone who wanted to pursue a speciality had to do their own original research.

Autoerotic Fatalities

Ressler and Douglas chose to pursue serial killers; Dick Ault dedicated himself to tackling terrorists, while Roy researched autoerotic fatalities – death from accidental strangulation or suffocation in search of sexual gratification. No one had taken the latter seriously with the result that many accidental deaths were mistakenly attributed to suicide. Even criminologists were curiously squeamish about discussing it. It was a taboo subject, something they believed needed to be cleared up, not understood. But as a result of Roy's intensive study both law enforcement and mental health agencies became aware of the extent of the problem, while many bizarre and mysterious deaths were readily explained and the cases closed.

Victims of this potentially fatal practice have died accidentally by hanging, from nitrous oxide poisoning and even from having the lower drawer in a chest of drawers pressing on their carotid artery while they were lying on the floor. Some even attempted to electrocute themselves and misjudged the voltage. It seemed there was no danger individuals would not risk in search of sexual excitement.

One man drove to a park in the middle of the night, dressed in female clothing and played the ultimate game of dare, Russian roulette, while pleasuring himself. No one knows how many times he had done this and survived. But when the police found the body in the back seat, he had evidently run out of luck.

It was Roy who came up with the distinctions organized and disorganized to describe the two main categories of serial killer, while collaborating on the influential article 'The Lust Murderer' with John Douglas in 1980. Typically, the top brass at the Bureau felt that this was too simplistic and insisted that they create a whole catalogue of categories such as Organized Asocial and Disorganized Nonsocial. But Hazelwood and Douglas' instincts proved right and today the distinction between a disorganized offender and an organized offender is sufficient to focus an investigation on the most likely suspects.

Roy admits that not all of his knowledge was obtained from training manuals or in the field. Some of the most valuable texts on profiling were novels such as *Crime and Punishment*, *The Angel of Darkness*, *The Alienist*, and *An Instance of the Fingerpost*. Another title Roy recommends for would-be profilers is *St Joseph's Children* which is based on a real case that he worked on. The perpetrator was a child killer who evaded the law for years by voluntarily entering a mental institution every time he sensed the police were closing in on him.

When asked what makes a successful profiler Roy will unhesitatingly answer, common sense. The second most important quality he says is lack of ego. Profilers work as part of a team and need to be receptive to other people's suggestions, to have respect for their specialist skills and experience. There is no place for the intuitive genius who demands that everyone must act on his hunches or visions.

The third attribute is experience. The fourth is the ability to detach oneself from the crime to ensure perspective in the same way that a surgeon or pathologist looks at their patient or a corpse as a subject to be worked on. The ability to think like the offender is lower on the list than one might imagine. But it is important to understand that this ability is not to be confused with getting into the offender's mind.

That is a conceit of popular fiction. A real profiler simply reasons as he imagines the offender will do. The big question he must ask himself is what would the UNSUB have done before, during and after the crime and what would he do now if he knew he was being sought.

When a psychiatrist expressed doubt that anyone could put themselves in the same mental state as a paranoid schizophrenic John and Roy offered to undertake a four-hour mental health test during which they would reason like the offender and give the answers they thought he would give. They were kept in separate rooms to ensure they didn't influence each other and at the end the psychiatrist who conducted the experiment diagnosed them both as classic paranoid schizophrenics.

The Evil That Men Do

The following exclusive interview with Roy Hazelwood was conducted by the author:

What part does intuition play in creating a profile?
Roy: If you have read my work, you have found that I list intuition as one characteristic that I look for in a good crime analyst (profiler). However, I go on to state that I don't believe there is any such thing as intuition, but simply use the term for lack of a better one. Let me explain. The human mind is the largest hard drive in the world and it has no delete button. In other words, we retain the memory of every experience in the recesses of our mind. If you doubt that, consider a person suffering senility may not be able to recall what happened 10 minutes ago, but can accurately describe what happened on a specific day when they were 10 years old. Consequently, I

believe that what we refer to as intuition is simply forgotten education and experience. Hence, when an intuitive analyst seemingly arrives at an opinion without conscious reasoning and we are all amazed, I believe that the analyst has simply taken in a number of variables, collated them, analyzed them, and then, based upon forgotten experiences and education, arrives at an accurate assessment within seconds.

What is the first thing that goes through your mind when surveying a crime scene? How do you begin to make sense from chaos?

Roy: It depends on the crime scene. If I am viewing the body of a murder victim, I may consider position, trauma, and state of attire. If I am viewing a scene, I may consider location, signs of struggle, and neatness or disorderliness of the scene.

As for the second question, I open a file on my computer and by reviewing the case documentation, viewing any photographs, and speaking with the investigator(s), I organize the information into various categories (i.e. victimology, trauma and/or autopsy, sexual assault, all geographic locations involved, any items taken, any indication of staging, etc.). Once I have captured all significant information, I am ready to begin my analysis of the crime.

Are there really urbane, sophisticated and educated killers out there or is this a fictional conceit?

Roy: Most of the serial offenders I have interacted with commit what John Douglas and I described as 'organized' crimes and are intelligent (not necessarily educated) offenders. The reason for this is simply that I only become involved in a case when the police have exhausted all major investigative leads with the offenders remaining unidentified. In most such cases those criminals are typically the more 'organized' and intelligent offenders.

Have you ever feared for your own safety or your mental wellbeing as a result of being exposed to these horrific crimes?

Roy: I have never feared for my mental wellbeing. I attribute this to the fact that I remember that my 'work' is not my 'life'. My work is what I do for an income and my life consists of my Christian faith, my family and my friends. This has proven to be successful for me over the years.

I have not feared for my safety but I recall being uncomfortable interacting with one particular offender while I was with the FBI's Behavioral Science Unit. This particular individual was a deputy sheriff while an active killer and we corresponded for a period of time. He had read a great deal of my writings and was very well versed in dangerous autoeroticism. I was uncomfortable interacting with this person because of the amount of influence he had over some male 'groupies' even though he was incarcerated. They were engaging in a variety of deviant behaviours at his direction and I felt it was not beyond the realm of possibility that he could direct an assault against me and consider it quite a coup too if it were successful. Obviously nothing happened and the man was subsequently murdered by another convict.

Author's note: The case Roy is referring to was that of Gerard John Schaefer, a former Florida police officer suspected of committing 29 murders. He was accused of using his official status as a pretext to get his victims into his car. He would claim he was arresting them, then drive out to the swamps, force them to drink laxative and beer because he got his kicks watching them defecate and urinate. Then he would force them at gunpoint to put a ladder against the nearest tree, climb up it and put a noose round their necks. Then he'd hang them. But the most disturbing aspect was that he would return some time later, dig them up and copulate with the corpses. But it got even more bizarre. When he couldn't find a victim, he would play the role himself. He would cross-dress and hang himself, and even photograph himself in the act.

What effect do such experiences have on the analyst (profiler) and how can they exorcize the images to which they are constantly exposed?

Roy: Every analyst is unique and each deals with the experience in their own way. However, I have worked with individuals who could not cope with the work and all subsequently left the field. One became a leading expert in an affiliated field, one became paranoid over the potential danger (largely imaginary) to his family and retired and two returned to criminal investigative work not dealing with violent crime.

Do offenders unconsciously harbour a desire to be caught?

Roy: I have never interviewed an offender who desired to be caught. Almost all but one wanted to be 'recognized' for what they had 'accomplished' but none wanted to suffer the punishment associated with being caught and convicted. Frequently a serial offender begins to take unnecessary risks and is caught. In such cases, it is hypothesized that the criminal had a subconscious desire to be caught. I personally believe that they begin to take unnecessary risks because they are narcissistic and, due to their criminal successes, begin to perceive themselves as invulnerable to identification and apprehension.

Theoretically we are all capable of murder if driven to an extreme, but are we all capable of premeditated murder?

Roy: If in fact we are all capable of murder if driven to an extreme, then it would follow that the more intelligent, emotionally controlled and organized person would plan the crime so as not to be caught. The more volatile person is certainly more likely to act spontaneously without premeditation.

If society lost interest in violent crime and the media more carefully controlled their coverage of such cases, would violent crime decrease or is this a modern 'disease' over which we have no control?

Roy: Of course society will never lose their interest and the media will not change their coverage policy in our lifetime.

Hypothetically however, I would surmise that a decrease could possibly occur. As previously mentioned, many of your violent serial criminals are narcissistic and crave attention. If attention was absent, it would remove one incentive for committing the crimes.

What is fundamentally 'wrong' with human beings that makes us capable of the inhuman acts observed over the years?

Roy: As a Christian, I believe in the inherent 'wrongfulness' of man and therefore the answer is quite simple for me. While I may hope for better behaviour, I don't expect better behaviour. However, leaving religion out of the equation, the entire world is in turmoil at this time and we are constantly confronted with a wide variety of unbelievable acts of violence. Our culture is awash with violence and our society is becoming more and more accepting and tolerant of its presence. Crimes that would have made headlines 40 years ago, are now found buried deep in the newspaper. It is very hard to shock the public and they are becoming apathetic. If we don't demand better behaviour, we will not see better behaviour. I will paraphrase the words of a famous English politician, Edmund Burke, who said, 'The only thing necessary for evil to succeed is for good men to do nothing.' Another famous personality, Albert Einstein, said, 'The world is a dangerous place, not because of those who do evil, but because of those who watch and let it happen.'

Is criminality a form of insanity or a character flaw?

Roy: Criminality is not a form of insanity. Criminality is a type of behaviour – illegal behaviour. In the US, insanity is a legal term indicating that the offender was not fully in contact with reality and therefore unable to distinguish between right and wrong, and consequently not legally responsible for his acts.

Are criminals born 'bad' or created by their upbringing?

Roy: Nature or nurture is an age-old question and one for which there is no proven answer to the best of my knowledge. I personally believe that it is more than likely a combination of the two.

How does one account for the disproportionate number of serial killers in the US?

Roy: There are multiple and complex reasons and the following are merely a few of those reasons.

First, the US has a very large population and occupies a very large geographic region. Second, there are no border controls within the United States and this allows unrestricted freedom of movement. Third, media coverage (e.g. movies, true crime books, crime novels, TV series, newspaper and television coverage of violent crime – specifically serial crime) is never-ending in the US. Fourth, media coverage of sex is never-ending and unavoidable in the US (e.g. advertisements, and the media coverage mentioned earlier). Fifth, the attention given to violent offenders and their crimes by the news and documentary industries is well beyond what is warranted (e.g. trial coverage, interviews of prosecutors, defence attorneys, jurors, surviving victims, and of course the offender himself). This amount of attention is very attractive to the narcissistic personality which is often found within the serial offender population.

Is our preoccupation with violent crime creating more serial killers?

Roy: In my opinion, the US public is preoccupied with serial crime as I have set forth in my answer to your previous question. However, I am not of the opinion that this preoccupation 'creates' serial offenders. Without question, it is appealing to the narcissistic criminal and therefore our preoccupation certainly impacts in some way.

Do law enforcement agencies generally work in concert with each other?

Roy: While there are still instances of proprietary interest among law enforcement agencies, I have found that there is a much better understanding of the absolute necessity to work together. I have found this to be particularly true in cases involving serial killers, serial rapists and child molestation.

Two excellent examples are available from the recent past. The first is the infamous Washington DC Sniper case. While I had no personal involvement in that series of shootings, I am aware of the wonderful co-operation between town, city, county, state and federal law enforcement agencies in that case. This excellent co-operation did not end with the arrest of the two responsible individuals, but extended over into their prosecution. The involved prosecutors met, exchanged information and agreed upon which jurisdiction would prosecute the individual cases.

Another example, and one in which I had some personal involvement in 2006, was a serial murder case involving the killing of seven prostitutes in Vancouver, Canada. The RCMP [Royal Canadian Mounted Police] there led a task force involving more than 30 investigators from three law enforcement agencies. This group had worked full-time together for over two years on the murders. I have seldom been as impressed with a co-operative effort as I was with this particular task force.

Have advances in forensic techniques and our knowledge of criminal behaviour increased the likelihood of apprehending and convicting the offender or have they created an unreasonable expectation of law enforcement?
Roy: The answer to both questions is a resounding yes. Law enforcement's ability to gain immediate access to nationwide fingerprint, ballistic and DNA data banks is resulting in the solving of an amazing number of violent crimes. The increased knowledge of personality and behavioural traits obtained from research of serial offenders lends itself to better investigative, interrogative and prosecutive strategies. This better understanding also lends itself to more effective proactive techniques as well as more effective searches of any property under the control of the offender. The negative aspect of this knowledge and methodology is that the public has developed the misperception that DNA, fingerprints or

ballistics are present in every crime. Furthermore, they don't seem to appreciate the fact that, even if the investigator has identified fingerprints, ballistics or DNA, it is not of much value unless there is an item or a person with which to match the material.

Another problem. Prosecutors are finding that jurors have these same misperceptions and this has proven to pose a problem in the trial process.

What single factor might reduce the incidence of violent crime or recidivism?

Roy: I can think of no single factor which would accomplish this task.

Is it possible to have empathy for offenders after witnessing the effects of their deeds?

Roy: One of the most interesting experiences of interviewing the offenders and their wives is the fact that most of them seem so 'normal' and, with rare exceptions, even likeable. As you are no doubt aware, many, if not most of them, had traumatic childhoods. When I am asked the question you have asked, my answer has to be yes, I have often felt empathy (not sympathy) for the offender. I like to say that my heart bleeds for them as children, however I absolutely hold them responsible for the criminal acts they committed. All of us are given choices as we move through life and our decisions determine the path our life takes. We are all responsible for the decisions we make and this is no less true for the violent criminal.

So, does your experience predispose you to hope or despair for the future of society?

Roy: I recognize that my work involves a relatively small segment of society. The vast majority of people I interact with in life are decent and hardworking people. I don't despair.

'None of us are saints.'
Albert Fish

References

The author wishes to acknowledge the following as primary sources of background material:

Britton, Dr Paul, *The Jigsaw Man* (Corgi 1998)

Britton, Dr Paul, *Picking Up The Pieces* (Bantam Press 2000)

Davis, Carol Anne, *Women Who Kill* (Allison and Busby 2002)

Douglas, John and Olshaker, Mark, *Mindhunter* (Mandarin 1997)

Douglas, John and Olshaker, Mark, *The Anatomy of Motive* (Pocket Books 1999)

Kelleher, Michael and Kelleher, C. L., *Murder Most Rare: The Female Serial Killer* (Dell 1999)

Keppel, Robert D., *Signature Killers* (Random House 1998)

Kessler, Ronald, *The Bureau* (St Martins Paperbacks 2003)

Lane, Brian, *Encyclopedia of Women Killers* (Hodder Headline 1994)

McCrary, Gregg O., *The Unknown Darkness* (Harper Torch 2003)

Paul, Jonathan, *When Kids Kill* (Virgin 2003)

Roland, Paul, *The Crimes of Jack the Ripper* (Arcturus 2006)

Roland, Paul, *Crime Scenes* (Arcturus 2006)

Roland, Paul, *The Nazis and the Occult* (Arcturus 2007)

Sereny, Gitta, *Into That Darkness: An Examination of Conscience* (Vintage 1983)

Vorpagel, Russell and Harrington, Joseph, *Profiles In Murder* (Dell 1994)

Website resources

http: www.crimelibrary.com

http: www.courttv.com

http: www.JohnDouglasMindhunter.com

http: www.fbi.gov

Index